POEMS, ESSAYS, AND OTHER WRITINGS

THE COLLECTED WRITINGS OF
MICHAEL JUSTE

IN TWO VOLUMES
VOLUME 2

TITLES IN THIS SERIES

POEMS, ESSAYS, AND OTHER WRITINGS

Michael Juste

THE WILD GANDER PRESS
MINNEAPOLIS—ST. PAUL

First published 1924–54.

ISBN 978-1-956796-11-7 (hardback); 978-1-956796-08-7 (paperback).

https://www.thewildgander.press

CONTENTS

Many Brightnesses

Miscellaneous Poems

Atomic Journey
A PLAY IN THREE ACTS

Short Stories

Essays

Reviews and Other Writings

NOTE ON THE TEXT

The present volume contains the poetry, essays, and shorter prose writings of Michael Juste, pseudonym of Michael Houghton; who also occasionally published under the nom de plume "QUAESTOR." Bibliographic details are given at the beginning of individual works, which, within each section, are organized chronologically by date of first publication. A small number of misprints and errors have been silently emended, citations have been updated, and a bibliography added. Otherwise the texts remain unchanged.

Escape, and Other Verse

DEDICATION

Dedicated to "M" (Brother to the World).
Who, from coloured threads of Truth,
Weaves a tapestry for Youth.

[Leeds: at the Swan Press, 1924.]

MYSTERY

The hushéd calls of night, the blue-framed moon,
The drift of clouds whose languid veils festoon
The old pale face that silvers night;
The sighing trees that glimmer white,
Traced by her wan cold beams.
Dim dreams reveal,
And ere they melt we gaze
In mute appeal.

And sad, ethereal tunes flow out from lips
Unseen, whose notes die with the dew that drips
From faerie stores of limpid wine,
Caressing ears with echoes fine.
So fine, they fade ere heard
Back to their spheres,
And 'mid the hush, our eyes
Are blurred with tears.

DEATH'S LAMENT

I heard Death mourn, "All things have rest,"
But I can never be God's guest,
Each spirit leaves its throbbing frame,
I free each faint imprisoned flame
From Life's clay cells.
My palace in a leafless wood
Stands wrapt in leafless solitude
Through windows wide far murmurs fall—
Man's mourning echoing through each hall,
And tolling bells.
I gather ashes, gather fears,
I gather lakes of human tears,—
Dark bitter waters deep as Time,
Fringéd with snow and ice and rime,
I harvest all.
The faery glow of lovely flowers
Whose perfumes flow from meads and bowers,
Has never draped my kingdom cold.
I but regale my eyes on mould,
On grave and pall.
Gaunt tombs and urns my gardens grow,
Pale sentinels in endless row,
Without one whisper save the wails
Of Agony's tear-laden gales
That sweep the land.

I heard Death moan; "The mortals quest
That they may earn eternal rest;
With sombre scythe I cut each thread,
My wages are the ash of dead,
Like grey, grey, sand.

Each bird, each bloom, each beast, each thing,
Greatest and least, finds sheltering.
Oh! I have seen their spirits rise
Great wingéd wonders to the skies,
On their last quest.
Though long ago I also trod
The flowery ageless realms of God.
My task can only end when I
Reap all the stars within the sky,
Then shall I rest."

AUTUMN'S SONG

Sip O flower Autumn's wine
Autumn's evening falls,
Now dissolve thy frail design
Ere cold Winter calls.

Melt to dust thy dainty dress,
Be the guest of Death,
Thy bee-crested gold recess
Crumble at my breath.

Fragrant fairy loveliness
Leaves her drooping frame,
Roams within the wind's caress
Like an unseen flame;
And her stem, her strength and sap,
Lie in grave of grass,
Dead, to sweeten Earth's green lap,
Till Time turns his glass.

*   *   *   *   *

She has faded: not a trace
Glows on Autumn's hem:—
Surely now that fragile face
Gems God's diadem.

THE URN

Man is a sealéd urn
Wherein fierce passions burn;
Whose walls throb to the sound
That travels round and round
From core of ruby flame,
The altar of man's frame,
Filled with the crimson wine
That builds up man's design.
But when the wine flows forth,
The urn's rent by the wrath
Of Death's grim hands and cold,
Then Beauty, robed in gold—
Comes where the urn lies low,
And hovering to and fro,
In subtle whisperings
Sings to the soul these things:
"The past was the unreal;
The urn could not reveal
The hidden realms that grace
And gem the deep blue space,
For man's dark urn of clay
Shuts out the richer day,
Until the hands of Death."

THE DEAD PLANET

In a dream I saw depart
An agéd globe,
With wisdom, life, and art,
And bloom-wrought robe.
Though vast, her golden frame
Dissolved away:
I heard her voice, ere flame
Melted her clay.
Her swan song roamed through space,
A sad, sad tune,
Ere lost in flame's embrace,
In fire festoon.
Her pools and seas breathed mist,
Her green tree-hair
Turned gold, and all atwist,
Became aflare,
Each peak with ruddy crest
Foamed into dust;
Her coloured curvéd breast
Was ashen crust.

And then, with clearer sight
I saw arise,
A host of souls in flight
For Paradise—
Pale faeries from their flowers,
Dim souls from streams,
Deprived of watery bowers,
Nymphs frail as dreams;
And ghosts from grove and wood,
Brown elf and faun,

Quaint shades that strayed or stood,
Dazed and forlorn.

    *   *   *   *   *

Then followed mankind's throng,
All space was lit:
Lastly, one god, whose song
Was "All is writ."

SONG OF THE SYLPHS

Come! O sisters of the skies!
Haste! the drooping blossom dies,
And each tree so faintly sighs
For our aery showers.

Hide with silver-fringéd veil
Where the gold-faced sun doth sail,
Pour o'er green-draped vale and dale
Wine for trees and flowers.

Hear, O sisters of the air,
Rising from the nymphs a prayer,
Weeping for their nectar share,
Fill their flower-decked ways!

Sister nymphs, drink deep, drink deep!
See the shining fishes leap.
Hear the music that we reap,
Low stream-psalms of praise.

THE MYSTIC'S VISION

Instead of stars I see calm faces shine,
Their bodies hid in dark blue seas of wine,
Each pouring forth a stream of melody
To all who unseal nature's treasury.

O who will drink with these old gods of gold?
Their faces smile and welcome all who hold
Great aspirations for a deeper life,
Unflawed by envy, self, or inner strife.

Come clime the ivory stairway of your soul,
And at its crest all beauty shall unroll.

ESCAPE

When Night, star-silvered, arches Earth,
And sheds her wistful calm,
My soul has then a richer birth
In lucent lands of charm.

I sight the gold-edged shores of dream,
And bathe in coloured foam;
And hear the scented winds that teem
With melodies that roam.

With godlike maids and men commune;
From God learn secret things;
But all grows faint—dream lore, dream tune,
When Earth's harsh daybell rings.

A QUESTION

Above the brink of dusk serenly came,
One uncompanioned argent light
Upon the marge of falling Night,
That entered with eternal spheres of flame—

Dim stars, in deepest blue enshrined, that shed
Thoughts of nobility and power
Within some minds that saw them flower;
Orbed symbols where God's wonders can be read.

Each star an unlinked letter of some word;
Each straying through apparent waste
In lonely beauty, calm and chaste,
In fire clad, like an ethereal bird.

What vast imagination did design,
And poured within those globéd forms,
The forces that through cosmic storms
Shaped perfect fruits to stream with silver wine?

WEARINESS

Could I but spill this flask of life,
And lose the pain of breath,
Becoming one with Death;
Flee from this world of haunting strife
Into a purer sphere
Where beauties dimly peer,
And robe my drowsing soul in chords
Of melting melodies,
And linger at my ease
On lovely, verdant, flowered swards;
And then still further rise
To some far Paradise,
Where deathless Spring pours out a wine
Unseen and soft as balm,
Filled with the golden calm
Of fair realms dewed with thoughts that shine,
Whose incense turns to fire
The soul, to soar still higher.

*   *   *   *   *

But vision darkens in the frost
Of melancholy's deeps;
Dreams fade as Sorrow reaps
The harvests of my soul; till, lost
From loveliness, I cry
To God, to let me die.

ECSTASY

I heard a bird when darkness shrouded me,
Sing from the brooding wood
Wherein I stood.—
The tresséd aisles turned golden; ecstasy
Sang through me; I dissolved,
And darkness rolled
To loveliness, and set my spirit free,

Green floor, wan sky, rushed into chanting seas
That robed vast spheres, that shone
As they swept on;
Then gushed cascades of regal melodies.
Each vivid giant star
Grew dim and far;
I was a mote in stilled eternities,

Where dwelt great spirits draped in lambent fire,
Who showered sparkling grain
That turned again
Through aeons, into stars born to expire.
They streamed with coloured glow
Like sands below,
Whose threads of song built up a cosmic choir.

I was all limpid light, whose flames gave birth
To hidden seas of gold,
That aureoled
The distant spheres; I was all love, all mirth,
All peace. Then died the light
My soul took flight;
Returning to this grain of sand called Earth.

WOODLAND MUSIC

They who wander in the woods,
Lingering 'neath leafy hoods,—
They have heard,
Voices murmuring aloft
And below, strange, subtle, soft,
Faint and blurred,
Sweeter than the branches sighs,
Or the bird-flutes in the skies,
Or the wind.
Listen keenly, all around,
Floats the timid, tangled sound,
Undefined.
Sensitive our souls must be,
Hushéd, lost in reverie,
Ere we lave
In the dim elusive tunes,
Flowing like magicians runes,
Wave on wave.

WINTER'S SONG

I breathe upon the clouds and change their rains into
      soft white showers,
That fall and hide all Autumn's art—her golden-
      tinted bowers
And fields, where grew her palaces of drooping,
      fading flowers.
Beneath my pale flocks falling from the cloud-
      enchanted air.
The Earth's dark eyes, the pools, gaze up with glazed,
      unwinking stare.
And hills are draped in petals, white like lilies,
      everywhere;
And leaf-shorn dryads slumber, and the nymphs
      within their streams.
I form a silver solitude webbed with the wan
      moonbeams,
And reign o'er frozen beauty while all faerie drink of
      dreams.

THE BLIND

If men but knew the hidden things
Behind the air, men would be kings.
Their eyes would see the gods of stars
Driving their orbéd flaming cars.
Whose foam of harmony would kiss
Their hearing with rich tones of bliss;
And holy perfumes they would drink
From Beauty's found and golden brink;
And they would burst their sealéd minds,
Rising on dreams as free as winds,
And all Imagination's store
Would colour Earth from shore to shore.
Their souls would be like harps, whose strings
Would quiver to the murmurings—
Of sleepy seas and solemn falls,
Of streams and tree-aisled forest halls,
All that they wished for would become
Their kingdom and Elysium.
If men had power to know the things
Behind the air, men would be kings!

Shoot—and Be Damned!

DEDICATION

Dedicated to Robert M. Reid,
whose views are similar to mine.

[London: Atlantis Bookshop, 1935.]

THE HUNGRY GUNS

War is declared,
And bands, prepared,
With brazen trumpets ring.
And strutting feet
March down the street
For country and for king.

The bugles blare,
And hearts aflare
Grow hot with lust to shoot,
The bugle's bray
Blows thought away
And wakes the primal brute.

The pipes are shrill
And blown with skill;
Like dying men they cry,
And as they pipe
The young and ripe
Rush into war to die.

The colours call,
So in they fall
Behind the flaunting flags;
Hurrah! they cry.
Then march to lie
A mess of bloody rags.

"We want your sons,
The hungry guns
Are waiting for their feast."

With roll of drum
 The soldiers come
To feed the martial beast.

The armies shake
 The towns awake
And tawdry tunes are roared.
 The horses rear,
 The gazers cheer
The glamour of the sword.

The songs are sung;
 The traps are sprung
Wherein death lies in wait.
 The streets grow still
 And hearts grow chill
That realise their fate.

THE SNARLING PUP

It was a dot upon a map
Began to show its teeth and snap;
A state so small, that no one knew
It stood until it came to view
Because a petty prince did laugh
At someone in the palace staff.
This was enough to set aflame
The country, for the princelet came
Upon another errand quite,
And so he set the state alight.
They quickly called the army out—
Five hundred men all strong and stout—
Who through the five-mile frontier dashed

And met the enemy and slashed;
Then, killing ten, returned to claim
That they had cleared the nation's name.
And here the great 'munition trust
Saw time was ripe to swiftly thrust
Upon the watching world the wars
That would relieve them of their stores.
They bade the eager waiting press
Write tales about their wickedness
The tiny state had had to stand
And suffer from the firebrand
And bully, who both day and night
Did vent its low and petty spite.
Thus all the papers with a shout
Said states must *not* be knocked about;
But as they wept about the weak,
Who were so innocent and meek,
A bigger nation quickly rose
And laid the state out in a doze
Of bombs and shells and whiffs of shot
Until the little state was not.
But they had done their duty for
The trusts that prepared THE war.

THE GOOSE STEP

Then countries, with a noble air,
Said: "Little nations must not bear
The bullying of bigger ones."
Therefore they also sent their sons,
Their aeroplanes, their cannons, tanks,
And lines of regimental ranks;
In millions conscripted for

The military game of war.
The military game that gulps
Strong men, then hideously pulps
Their forms into a bloody mess:
Torn forms of nightmare ugliness.
Then all the nations swiftly found
That they were very neatly bound;
That during peace the states had planned
How thoughts of freedom could be banned;
How every movement was forestalled;
How each was a number called;
How everyone was placed in line;
How even sneezes brought a fine.
How smiling babies in their cots
Were fed in well disciplined lots.
That sharp at six all had to rise
To listen to the radio lies;
And they who rose a moment late
Would meet a sharp, unpleasant fate—
Examples to the foolish folk
Who had imagined war a joke.
On every wall was fixed a sheet
That told of how and when to eat.
And everyone received a book
That told of how and when to look,
And what to do and where to go
In case invaded by the foe:
And where to work and where to walk;
And words to use in time of talk.
All of the little bureaucrats
Now flourishéd like well-fed rats
Clothed in their "brief authority,"
They stamped on the majority;

They placed each person in a cage
And swiftly flew into a rage
If one would dare to answer back;
Their faces would grow blue and black,
And order them into a spot
Where they would probably be shot.
They were the fingers of a might
That now could freely scratch and bite.
So freely did they scratch and tear
And place their trademark everywhere.

*   *   *   *   *

Now brooding Hate, so long athirst,
Upon the waiting planet burst;
From platform and from press he roared
That all should use the gun and sword.
And, if not fight, shake fists at those
Who could not rush upon their foes.
Hate rushed amok and slimed the brain,
And almost turned the good insane;
Mild men who never dreamed that they
Could wish to bayonet and slay,
Were poisoned by Hate's venom till
They foamed and raved and longed to kill.
None would have cared if all the old;
Whose minds were dead, whose hearts were cold
Were mangled by the hate they wrought,
But happy youth was also caught.

THE THUG LET LOOSE

Then politicians, once quite small,
Boomed by the press, became quite tall;

And all their vices, once suppressed,
Were now completely unrepressed.
The foul, the mean, the human lice,
Who love to prey on human vice;
The thug, the poisonous, the scum,
The sadist and the mental dumb
Were now allowed full play, and so
They roused each race to fight the foe.
Now everywhere their voices pealed
To urge men to the battlefield;
They leered and bullied, lashed the whips
Of evil words from evil lips.
They strutted here, saluted there;
They planned and plotted everywhere.
Their warped and warlike manners sent
The thoughtless to a regiment.
Recruiting there, recruiting here,
They martialised the atmosphere,
In uniforms and very proud
They won the clamour of the crowd;
For crowds love leaders who are crude
And blustering and somewhat rude.
And so they swiftly fell in line
In order that the guns could dine.
Quite gladly did they let the pest
Become the leaders of the West;
Become the leaders till their world
Back into chaos would be hurled.

THE PRESSTITUTES

Then all the press lords, quick to gain
A fortune from a people's pain,

Leaped into action with a shout
And shot their printed venom out;
Used all their psychologic arts;
Pumped hate and poison into hearts
Until all morals grew oblique;
Wove tales about the poor and weak,
And bid the people rise and haste
To guard and keep their women chaste;
They did not know their enemies
Lived right amid their families;
A menace that ruled thought and speech
Although remaining out of reach;
A power that increased its loot
Awhile it urged the world to shoot;
A power to whom war and crime
Was better than a peaceful time
When man could raise a nobler state
And be the master of his fate;
A power that grows fat on death,
On guns and fumes that poison breath;
A power seeming to deny
Divinity that dwells on high.
With extra that and extra this
The press lords licked their lips in bliss;
Ten times a day they printed news,
And added lies when lacking news.
"Prepare for war, prepare to fight,"
(Prepare to spread through earth a blight.
Prepare to mangle man to rags,
And fill your hungry money bags.
Prepare to hide the world in clouds
Of poison gas. Prepare the shrouds.)
"Prepare," comes forth from every press.

(And smear out Nature's loveliness.)
Poor simpletons! they did not see
That war now lay in chemistry;
That war had moved at such a pace,
It could annihilate the race;
That scientists could move so fast
And blow the world back to the past.
They did not think that war would sweep
The world into a rubbish heap;
They did not think that they would share
The poisons floating through the air;
That profiteers, despite their greed,
Would hungry vermin fatly feed.
That king and queen and duke and lord
Would level lie with all the horde
Of commoners; that everywhere
The stench of death would foul the air.
None would escape: French, Germans, Jews,
Chinamen, Negroes and Hindus,
Arabs, Greeks and Cingalese:
Black, brown, yellow families
In all their millions would yield
Their bodies to the battlefield.
In all their millions would lie
And no more blaring papers buy.

THE EVIL TRIAD

Then all the nations loudly cried:
"We must preserve our country's pride;
We must preserve the world from those
Who once were friends but now are foes;
With poison gas, with bomb and gun

We must destroy them—everyone."
And with them yelped the yellow press
Revealing all the nakedness
Of evil that the enemy
Would bring to earth so frightfully.
In words of crimson posters flared;
In words of black the columns blared;
In pictures of such bestial shapes:
One thought the enemy were apes,
But far more brutish: low as mud;
A race whose joys were spilling blood;
A race gorillalike and rude,
In whom the grimmest evil brewed.
A race so bad, that readers gaped
And wondered how they had escaped
Before the press revealed the sin
That walked amid their kith and kin.
Then old men rose, and, with a shout
Began to drive the young men out;
Their noble paunches and their jowls
Quivered amid their wheezing howls;
Shook in their hurricane of hate
That urged the young men to their fate.
Full nobly did the old men wave
The flag that symbolised the grave
In foreign soil: a death that flattened
And foreign vermin richly fattened.
A death by flame that turned young men
Into a shape one could not pen.
A death by bomb that spread so far
The body from the fields of war;
It made it international;
And this would have been rational

If this conception had but hit
Their brains before they "did their bit."
A subtle death: a death by vapours,
Wherein they danced fantastic capers,
And then in swift paralysis
Melted beyond analysis.
A death by gun; a death quite clean,
They were, and then they were not seen.
A death by plague where bacilli
Revealed a hundred ways to die;
That knew no rank and crossed the line
And there impartially did dine.
A death by mud: a mud that stank
With soldiers flesh of every rank.
That down the choking throat did slip
As clawing hands dead bones did grip.
A death for heroes, who again
Possessed brave hearts but little brain.

*   *   *   *   *

Yet every death did mean increase
In circulation and in ease
For press lord and for profiteer,
Whose wives, white feathers, with a sneer
Gave to those men whose saner views
Conflicted with their lying news.
And old men drove their petty clerks,
But kept the typists at the works,
Who, free from friends and husbands, learned
How easy money could be earned;
That cash, piled up from shells and guns
That battered everybody's sons,
Could bring bright jewels in a flood:

They rarely thought they grew from blood.
But some men walked in uniforms—
Although afar from metal-storms
That shrieked about the smoky air—
They mixed with ladies rich and fair
Who knitted woollen socks for those
Who still remained upon their toes.
Here, quite erect, in soldier style,
They handed tea and won a smile;
Then talked in solemn tones of men
Who laid aside the pick and pen
In order that their shares could fly
As high as shells within the sky.

THE MORONS

And they who let injustice reign,
And were indifferent to pain
That other nations had to bear:
Who did not raise a hand to spare
The agony that broke the brain
The soul and body in the strain.
All those indifferent people who
Thought war was like a great tattoo,
To gaze upon and gaily clap
Were also flung into the trap,
To find that military shows
Were very painful, when the foes
With undiscriminating shell,
Produced a pyrotechnic hell.
A show that shot them into pieces,
Mothers, fathers, nephews, nieces:
An audience that learned too late

That war was not at all a féte.
And all of those who did not know
That very soon a war would blow
Their little hobbies and their arts,
Into a million little parts;
Their little comforts and their games
Into the agony of flames;
Their little bowler hats and bags,
Their little habits and their fags;
Their daily trips into the works
As typists, travellers and clerks.
Who thought all politics a bore;
Who did not care what lay in store;
Whose rabbit brains quite smugly read
And held to what the papers said:
These dull nonentities whose sense
Could see no further than their fence
That ringed their little garden plot,
Were unaware they soon would rot.
And they who dreamed that struggling man
Would in the future shape a plan
When they would harness the machine
And make our lives all calm and clean,
Were also shattered by the claws
Of martial might, and all its laws.
Were broken as their broken hearts—
For war treads down the peaceful arts;
Stamps into ruins what is fair;
Annihilates the rich and rare;
Its crimson mind and flaring soul
Despises the pacific role.
Thus hand in hand with trusts and banks
It turned the ploughshares into tanks.

Whilst scientists, whose years of toil
Discovered how to fight and foil
Some venom that the world might live,
Reverted to the primitive,
And carefully researched to find
A way to blow up humankind.
Thus brilliant brains that could have hurled
The war lords to their sunless world,
Had they but organised and said
They would not load the Earth with dead,
Mixed grim explosive gases till
They found a deadlier way to kill.

LET US PREY

And from the press the constant bawl:
"Obey your noble country's call."
Prepare to die, prepare to fight;
Prepare 'munitions day and night.
Prepare to cheer the marching ranks
And chase and beat the peaceful cranks.
Prepare to drown them in a howl
Who dare to say that war is foul,
And duck them in a nearby ditch;
For they disturb the would-be rich,
Who now can raise the price of bread
In honour of the mangled dead.
For they remembered that the last
Great war brought them a great repast;
When food became so scarce that they
Could make the common people pay.
And so destroy the pacifist;
For they are few and can't resist.

Prepare to scowl, prepare to storm
At those who wear no uniform.
Prepare to let your feeble soul
Be fevered by war's foul control.
Prepare to let it leap within
And stir you to the foulest sin
Of killing brothers, sisters, sons
Through bombs and poison gases, guns.
And yet prepare to raise this curse
Within the sound of holy verse,
Where unctuous brothers of the cloth
Will bless your military wrath:
The cleric, suave and sinister;
The coward-minded minister
Whose elocutionary wind
Will hide the thoughts within his mind:
"Oh, God, from Whom all blessings flow,"
("Please pulverise the hated foe.")
"In whom we have our life and breath,"
("Oh may they have a hideous death.")
"To Whom we humbly kneel and pray,"
("That young man *there* avoids the fray.")
"Give us this day our daily bread."
("The papers say: 'Ten million dead.'")
"And let us sleep secure and sound."
("May all the enemy be drowned.")

THE CROAKERS

Prepare to read the latest lies,
And look about for furtive spies;
Prepare to hear the radio
Announce new horrors of the foe,

And hear Professors prove to you
That everything you heard was true:
That they could prove by history
That blood was drunk instead of tea;
That through the ages they did eat
Poor infants when they wanted meat;
And listen carefully to this,
Then rise, and swear your greatest bliss
Would be to hear them when they boil
Within great pots of sizzling oil.
And then, providing you are old,
Prepare to look alert and bold,
And if you have strong lungs, prepare
To make your audiences share
The hate you feel, and then denounce
The young who will not haste to pounce
Upon the enemy who are
Abroad, and, safely, very far.

THE BEAST AMOK

The battlefield comes to the street;
It lies in wait where lovers meet.
Where churchbells ring to slanting stones
Recording prayers to dust and bones,
The battlefield comes even there
To shatter graves and stench the air.
The battle through still cloisters comes
With roar of bombs and boom of drums.
Within each heart the battle spreads
And everywhere a hatred sheds,
Within each brain the evil flares;
Helped by the papers with their scares;

The papers that for pennies strive
To keep the beast in man alive.
To villages of peace and charm
The battle stretches out its arm,
And in its fiery fingers smears
In smoke the lovely art of years.
From land to land and sea to sea
The battle rages thirstily:
It runs amok, it blindly raves
And strikes the press lord and his slaves;
With tanks and bombs and planes and guns
It slays the daughters and the sons
Of heartless men who did not care
As long as they increased their share:
Those unseen criminals who bought
Sly ministers in every court.
Unknown, unheard, they held the reins
And quietly increased their gains.
Whilst youthful patriots who read
Of deeds wrought by heroic dead,
Whose blood ran fast, who thought how fine
To win v.c.'s and lead the line,
Found modern war was not quite fair
As they went flying through the air;
Found war was not at all a game
Before they died by gas and flame.
And where the battlefield rolls on
All faith in God and love is gone.
And madness grips and all fulfil
The grim command to go and kill.
To watch with burning eyes the blood
Of friend and foe rise in a flood,
And then to fall with rattling breath

Into the holocaust of death.
To cut and thrust, to rape and rend,
To see the entrails of a friend
Lie mixed with quivering bits of one
Who was another nation's son.
To drink, until with maddened brain
They rush into the fight again:
Poor, blinded brutes made bestial by
The callous powers who bade them die;
The callous powers who do not care
How many die or when or where.
The callous powers whose souls are dead;
Whose minds are black, whose hearts are lead.
Who put the world upon the rack
And bring the Middle Ages back.
The polished primitives who rule
And all the simple people fool.
The battlefield does not draw down
A line 'twixt commoner or crown.
The battlefield is cruel and blind
And has no heart for humankind;
Its scythe is merciless and sweeps
Whatever walks or flies or creeps.

THE CABINET DISSOLVES

Then cabinet had barely met
To weave their tangled, verbal net,
To gravely ponder how to win,
When from the air there rose a din;
It sounded like a fleet in flight:
The enemy had come in sight.
And ere the cabinet could fly

The cabinet began to die.
Thus in a firework display
The cabinet sailed right away.
Quite loftily the premier rose,
And all his noble phrases froze:
Phrases quite dignified, though blurred
In thought, but clear in every word.
Thus like a meteor he flew
And would have had a bird's-eye view
Of citizens within the flames
Who cursed his kind in bitter names.
But he was definitely dead:
His black tail coat was widely spread;
Quite like a bird he swiftly soared,
Perhaps to stand before the Lord
To answer why he had not striven
To bring to Earth a touch of Heaven,
Instead of giving full control
To men without a touch of soul;
To obscene brutes whose code and creed
Lay in an ever-growing greed.
And with him came a noble lord;
Who thought of wars in bow and sword:
Romance in battle was his passion;
But he was forced to follow fashion.
Thus, though his mind dwelt in the past,
He detonated in a blast
Shot from a plane, the latest one:
And so he progressed at a run.
Then followed at his flying feet
The admiral of all the fleet;
Who swore quite horribly as he
Rose right above his enemy:
He somersaulted up and on;

His blazing form with medals shone,
To dive amid the hungry fish
And there become a tasteless dish.
And then a minister of state
Came following at quite a rate;
With sheets of paper everywhere
Of plans to make the people share
The cost of war by buying tons
Of War Loan that would purchase guns;
And on new generations lay—
Long after war had passed away—
An interest so heavy that
The people would lose all their fat,
And grow so thin, that they would pause
And wonder why they entered wars.
Then like dark rooks within the sky
The secretaries hurried by:
Well-groomed and sleek, who hoped to rise
And lead the nation's destinies.
They did not dream to rise so quick;
And thought this was a nasty trick.
For years they were prepared to wait
To rule as captains of the state.
Alas! this eager waiting list
Was instantaneously dismissed,
Perhaps to bring the message to
The Devil waiting for the crew,
That they were quite prepared to be
The servants of his majesty.
So this exclusive gathering
Through foreign arms went scattering;
Although some shells, and these not dud,
Had been produced by local blood.
Perhaps the very shell that raised

A minister, was by him praised
Before it left the land to be
A weapon for the enemy.
So scattered over all the realm
Lay fragments of the nation's helm.

THE DIE-HARDS

Then where the old men bawled: "We must
Pound all the enemy to dust."
Great clouds of poison gas descended
And all their poison speeches ended.
So they inhaled what they had bred
And also joined the mass of dead.
And journalists, who used the pen
To keep ablaze the hearts of men,
Were quite as painfully destroyed
As all the victims they decoyed;
Their lives were just as quickly snuffed
As priest and profiteer they puffed.
And ladies, proud, who though superior,
Were kind to soldierly inferior,
Were also mingled with the slain
And mixed their blood within the drain.
Whilst little girls and little boys
Who played with military toys
Now saw the bigger ones ere they
Were blown to pieces whilst at play.
A pity, but their parents shared
The deadly views the papers blared;
The deadly views they helped to build
And make all Earth a battlefield.
They helped to glorify the beast

And threw their offspring to the feast:
The little ones, the lame, the blind,
The ugliest, loveliest of mankind.
Too cowardly, too dim in brain
To know that if they fought again
That they, their children, all the world
Into perdition would be hurled.

THE PATRIOTS

And they who sat and fiddled thumbs
And said they loved the sound of drums;
Who rose with martial ardour when
The country cried: "We want more men."
So into factories they tore
To help to add the fuel of war,
And also money till it raised
Them up to heights where they were praised.
They also followed; for the gases
Killed the cunning as well as the asses.

*   *   *   *   *

And bishops, sleekly round and grave,
Who blessings very freely gave
Within the cathedrals quiet and dim,
Who led with holy psalm and hymn,
Lay strewn about the pews and aisles
In queer and unbeatific styles.

POT-POURRI

And gentle ladies, sweet and kind,
Who fed the poor and helped the blind,

41

Who did not dream nor ever knew
Their money from gun-metal grew,
That in a not far distant day
Ten thousand lives would blast away—
Their brokers gave them good advice,
So money came and things were nice—
Lay smeared amid their charming rooms
Mixed up with tea things, texts and blooms.
Whilst firemen in helms of brass,
Lay torn amid bombed brick and glass:
'Mid hose their scattered bodies sprawled;
They could not help the ones who called.

THE LAY-OUT OF THE LAST EDITOR

And editors, whose only shot
Was stern and solemn sounding rot,
In heavy Sunday articles,
Were also blown to particles.
About the splintered bits of dead
Their verbal flatulencies spread,
And, added to the foeman's drive
Slew those who might have been alive.
Distributed amid his press,
A press lord looked a greasy mess;
His "innards" dangled from the roof;
His brains lay mixed with ink and proof;
The head that plotted war and hate
For petty pence, now met his fate.
His legs were jellied on the platen;
They made a most unpleasant pattern;
Awhile his bulky body lay
All ripped to pieces by the spray

Of red hot metal from the sky—
His was an ugly way to die.
An hour before—all cock a whoop,
He had prepared his greatest scoop:
A lie so venomous and foul,
It would have made the country howl:
Till even agéd men would run
From bath chairs with a bomb or gun.

THE PROFESSOR GETS IT

Professor Blite, a blameless man,
Was busy with a wholesale plan;
A bomb quite small, and yet so vast
In power, that within a blast
A city could dissolve away
Like wax within the heat of day.
This scientist: Professor Blite
Worked at his bomb by day and night;
His lofty brow looked quite benign,
One did not think it could design
Explosives that could atomise
His friends as well as enemies.
One element alone he lacked;
It came, when they were all attacked,
And from a foreign student fell
A bomb that shot him into hell.

THE WASTE

A week before a gracious wood
Beyond a happy village stood.
A hundred years had nature striven

To make this wood a misty haven,
Wherein the birds could nest and sing
The songs the boughs were whispering.
A hundred years, and in a day
The birds were blown to feathered spray;
The wood was sick, the glade was bare;
For many bodies rotted there;
Whose sightless eyes stared at the flowers;
Whose blood lay with the dews and showers
And where the village bell had sung,
The hands were dead that woke its tongue.
The fruit trees ripened with the wheat,
But no one came to pluck and eat;
A different fruit fell from the sky,
And thus the villagers did die.

TALE OF A RAT

Within a glade of tropic palms,
Away from war and its alarms:
A rat quite sleek and strong and stout
From a fat stomach clambered out:
A larger rat, a human one,
Whose shares lay in a massive gun—
Long distance range—whose screaming shell
Gould dig a crater deep as hell,
Lay rotting there. This beast with brains
Believed that in these hot domains,
Five thousand miles from skyey death
That poisoned air and tortured breath.
He would escape, and, nestling there,
The tropic entertainment share.
Alas! one thing he had forgot:
That winds could bear this poison rot;

That winds could carry to his heart
The foulest poisons of man's art.
And so he lay, yet lived again
Within a rat of nobler strain.

SACNTUS, SANCTUS, SANCTUS

The vesper bells rang hushedly
Above a twilit nunnery;
They ran so virginal and soft:
They lifted all the souls aloft
Until their senses seemed to swim
Within the sweetness of each hymn.
The halo of the holy hour
Encircled them as in a flower
Whose hidden petals scented all
The nunnery from wall to wall.
But as they kneeled and prayed there curled
The fumes from out the warring world;
The fumes that turned the tender hymn
Into a dreadful requiem,
Until in agony they cried
To Blessed Mary, ere they died;
Awhile above them stood and gazed
The cross and Christ they daily praised.

ASHES TO ASHES—

Everywhere the fumes came pouring;
Everywhere the guns went roaring;
Everywhere the towns lay shattered
And their citizens lay battered.
Everywhere the martial races
Lost their higher human traces;

Sinking swiftly, sinking nearer
To their savage, primal era
When their hearts and heads were bestial,
Knowing nought of the celestial.
All the centuries of learning
Melted in a mighty burning;
All that loving hands had nourished;
All the beauty that had flourished;
Works as delicate as petals;
Finely beaten lustrous metals:
Artists who had starved to fashion
All the splendours of a passion.
And cathedrals, grave and lofty,
Wherein mellow organs softly
Paeaned praises, also perished
With the altars that they cherished.
Whilst their portly deans and deacons
Watched them rise away in beacons.
Priests, whose shares were also booming
As the aeroplanes went zooming.
Everywhere the air grew sickly
With the fumes that poisoned quickly:
Heavy vapours, strong and vivid
Turning everybody livid.
Everywhere were voices shrieking
From the gas masks that were leaking;
Whilst their hands with frantic gripping
Tore the flesh the fumes were ripping.
Through the burning streets went raving
Those who hours before were waving
Flags and signing songs of hatred,
Caring nought for what was sacred.
All their burning tongues and terrors
Could not rectify their errors.

DUST TO DUST—

The war blazed on: a fiery lash
That shrivelled everything to ash.
The fool, the sage, the strong, the weak,
The innocent, the good, the meek.
It slew the child, the women, and
The Trust that all the murder planned,
Through Europe, Asia, U.S.A.
It swept the nations in the fray.
Through jungles, seas, and through the air
It hurled its evil everywhere.
Till Nature rose in rage and broke
The final clutches of man's yoke.
With famine, flood and plague she ran
And helped to end what guns began.
Right back to the primordial state
The world rushed at a frantic rate.
Till everything grew sweet and clean,
And man no longer stained the scene.

R.I.P.

The Earth was happy now, and freed
From engineering bonds and speed,
Gave better things a chance to rule
Beside her vanished two-legged fool:
Like beetles, butterflies and dogs,
Hyaenas, hares and bugs and frogs.
Back to the primitive she turned,
Her lesson well and truly learned:
That never in a future age
Would man be centre of the stage.

47

Many Brightnesses

DEDICATION

To Doreen with love.

[London: Neptune Press, (1954)]

A MOMENT'S VISION

And magic, too, see there:
I press the pen, the page grows golden grain,
A surge of words: waves from my mind—
The doors of thought flung wide.

This stuff is swift and sweet.
I am an archer now: the target?—God.
The arrow strikes: ah cataract of love!
Descending bliss and anodyne. Ah rich good rain!
All bitter swept away.

Upwards I glance:
The sky's all crystal; bright with prophecy.
An altar amid corybantic clouds,
Heaven in dance, in revelry.
The altar burns with God.

MANY BRIGHTNESSES

A LOVE CYCLE

I

A lotus eater when the twilight flowers
With delicate gardens: avenues of air
Wherein my thoughts move softly. Here shy bowers
Breathe odours for the loitering mind. I share
Love's many brightnesses, in bloom and vine
For my soul's eyes; love's cadences awake,
Smile from the heart's deep; glances that intertwine
With tendrilling touch.
Gently I slake
My hungers on these shades; elusive fruit
Ere evening's Lethe flows and all grows mute.

II

Fair fire of my soul and grace of good:
My lambent love: surge of my ardent mood.
From my heart's furnace to my secret star
And its embracing brightness from afar:
In brooks of praise: in cataracts of song
To streams of exaltation: swiftly, strong,
I sing love's rich beatitudes: I greet
Gazelle of God laved in love's paraclete.
Helen, Beatrice and sad Persephone,
All, all exalted were, and I—exalt but thee.

III

The heart's a hermitage with one lone lover;
When Spring's ajar the heart new loves discover.
The heart's awhistle when the air's a-rustle;
And amber April sets the birds a-bustle.

The heart's a hidden spire the green hours pealing,
Hours of the fragrant rains redolent with healing.
The heart's an emerald Eden a fair Eve sharing
Wherein God walks again when love's declaring.

IV

And many brightnesses hath love: now moods
Of silver courtesies, now golden floods
Of adoration, or slow amber dawns
Of love unfolding: thoughts like dappled fawns
Hiding in summer coverts drowsily
Or noons of tenderness. Love's dynasty
Is the soul's flame radiant from root to flower
In growing grace and firm uplifting power;
Raising us high from earth and its despair
To hidden Eden's amaranthine air.

V

Love's many brightnesses—its gentle pride,
A steadfast star whose beams embrace the bride.
Its quest: a rose of iridescent fire
Held high in sweet defiance and desire.
Its gentleness: twin soothing hands to heal
And eyes compassionate. What can conceal
All this diffusing blaze? From Paradise
To Erebus' glow, from calm exulting skies
To ash and ember in the deepest pit,
Great love remembers and is ever lit.

VI

I send you love;
See how the petals glow,
Its trembling calyx gleams and dewily;

If I could be all crystal, love would show
The troubled heart of me.

VII

And love's bright hierarchies: they ever keep
Sweet vigilance, with wings that ward and sweep
About this dual bliss: with shining swords
About this blaze of love, guard lover's lords.
And bright the blessed bower for this tryst:
Love garlanded amid a golden mist:
Love bright with fragrant singing—praising each
With lips as censers, love the myrrh of speech
Until from altars of their hearts they give
The attars of their loves and richly live.

VIII

And now love's nimbus coloureth each part
With gentle fires from shining head to heart:
Azures of tenderness to bind the bliss
Warm coral tints to aureole each kiss:
And clasping hands in coif of crystal gold:
Vestments of love that flicker and enfold—
A hymn of hues: soft psalms of radiant pearl,
Fair tapestries of anthems, coil and whirl
In rainbow exultation; every zone
One choiring chord and one ecstatic tone.

IX

Love, that had bound
The reason in a wreath
Of roses, found
Great sorrow underneath.
The thorns had bruised

After the buds had blown,
And reason, loosed,
Unhappy, walked alone.

X

The many brightnesses of love: bright tears
Welling from a wild grief, the burning rain
Of love's grey hopelessness, a lover's fears
Love's Calvary whence we arise again
From crown of thorns, from torturing cross.
Into translucent light: the gift of grief
To exultation—victory from loss:
Brightness from ash and anguish. Yet too brief
This flight of flame; Gethsemane returns
But to the heart—brightness more gently burns.

XI

Now in the dove-light of the dusk I hear
A gossamer music: tender benison
For the bruised heart: ripple of atmosphere
In tones of gentle grey, shadowily wan.
Love's brightnesses—beneath the nocturne's spell—
Drift like a pastel pageant of regrets—
Sad unfulfilments, ebb and flow of bells.
Echoing voices—the heart's forgotten debts:
Fine nuances of sound that shyly ease
The inner hurt, the wraiths of memories.

XII

Love haloes all: linking the dove to rose
In emerald clouds; the minuet of wings
To stately flowers, the winds with nectar blows
Amid this secret carnival and brings

55

Love's amber brightness. All is magical
To vision's calyx: the seer's sight unfurled
Beholds from zone to zone earth's festival:
Cities and seas and mountains of the world
In one soft glow of God. Love over all
In heights and deeps—one tender coronal.

SYNTHESIS

Now I will gather in the hues of heaven
To mix with tints of May and waxing June
And bring their brightnesses to Love's soft leaven
Till inner night returns to inner noon.
Love makes all luminous: the secret places
Where Judas dwells to strike the John in me,
For spring is grained with paradisal traces
And love unlocks the griefs that girdled me.
Apocalyptic moment of my being,
Love's golden synthesis: all heart, all seeing

THE SUCCUBUS

From the deep fires of darkness was I whelped;
Amid the shouts of hell and the beat of hoofs;
All the caverns aroar;
Crept I from a cocoon of scales.
And the tusks of my father in gape and grin.
Many curses did my mother whisper into my ears;
And my father spat venom into my mouth.
And a fever was set about my thighs
And twin vampires within my breasts,
And my arms were pythons.
Yet in the dream of man I am a flame, and fair,
For I wear their visions:
In veils of gold and silver I hide
As they sing hymns to my hell.

HECATE

From withering throne—the waning moon—
I thread the thought and slily spin
Slanting pattern of spell and rune,
And sow the night with sin.

Then covens greet and pirouette
Beneath the sulphur of the air,
And witch and warlock minuet
Amid my tangled hair.

The crypts and caverns wake and wail
And thin hobgoblins prance.
"Queen Hecate," they shrill and hail,
"Come lead the Sabbat dance."

The whinnying hurricane my steed,
A crimson cloud my robe,
I whirl my diabolic breed
About this slumbering globe.

LOOTERS OF MAN

Nonentities bright priests,
Acolytes of iron;
Immutable, soulless,
Over mankind cowled in brass
And rivetted to robot law
In adamant abattoirs
Or plastic cathedrals;
Where the smooth rods of logic rule;
All intellect and polished order,
And reason's shining bars;
Oiled noiseless speed
And passionless glass;
Minds of steel:
Machines jerking,
Alloyed fingers dancing,
Imagination's rainbow scrubbed:
Made barren, grey
Or sightless black:
Emotions nailed, stamped, boxed;
Neatly diced in technicolour slabs.
Artificial arts:
Epileptic jets of jazz:
Notes gulped by cogged wheels:
Clattering loud orisons
In a surrealistic glare.
Brittle odours, fumes:
Staccato carnival:
All hope vivisected—
A clinical Pantheon
With gods of chemistry as Lords.
Lustless and lustreless:

Mechanical Prometheans,
But of all man the heart
Pecked by eagle Despair.
Or, earth one Setebos;
Metallic Caliban the king
Crabwise asprawl:
Fists of girders, cranes:
Fragmentising mind
To one granite level

UNITY

Here I hold within my hand
Grains of shining silver sand;
But the mistiness of sight
Cannot see these worlds aright.

Then into the sky I stare;
Other sands are shining there
Scattered in a golden shower
By a vaster, unseen power.

Yet these worlds below, above,
Are united in the love
Wherein ecstasy descends
And each separate atom ends:

Making earth and sky and sun
Sand and star and soul all one

MICROCONSCIOUSNESS

The knotted universe expands;
Atomic entities record
Philosophies, and chant of lands
   Where light is Lord.

Our shafts of sense probe through the deeps
Into our many-mindedness
Where chaos into pattern leaps
   To loveliness.

The minute music of the spheres
Upon the sunken senses break
And lo! the Macrocosm hears
   A world awake.

REGAL DAYS

Ah! light-lapped regal days who held long trysts with
    me;
Who clad my sallow hours with crystallinity:
When through the haggard years an April music
    woke
Whose syllables of spring in singing voices spoke.
And sometimes through the night, the samite of a
    star
Wreathed round my heart and comforted with vi-
    sions from afar.

FROG POND

CARTOONS IN VERSE

I. FROG POND

In every part they sit
And quack. Its few have wit
And few have fervent fire;
And many love the mire.
Grotesques, with little grace,
Each has his little place.
And I am one with all—
And also small.

II. BOHEMIAN CAFÉ ON SATURDAY

This is a twisted place: bubbling babble, stale,
Sly fingered, weasel-tinged. Here sits a pale
Brass-headed prostitute, whose glance
Jeers at a giggling group from some late dance:
Flushed, gay and scented near two pimps who stare:
This is the home the street's night-gypsies share
For warmth and crafty company: café
Where simple artless feed the artful stray.
The unkempt thought grows richly here, unchecked
Goes rioting, and—ultimately—wrecked:
The inward ill-at-ease, the incomplete,
The crank, the student, the pervert, the effete,
A pattern of blurred colours, steam and smoke:
A cartoon of the world's abnormal folk.

Some shy suburbans quietly wander in
To gape and dabble furtively in sin.
Neuroses fall and tight repressions burst:
This place can satisfy all forms of thirst.

Six days respectability remains:
Comes Saturday and the Libido reigns.

III. A BOOKSTALL'S MONOLOGUE

The scramble's on, and furiously dart
A web of frantic hands about the mart
Of pompous folios and cloth-bound chatter:
The meat of minds and many without matter.
There's Reverend Dripnose with his rheumy eyes;
A twittering man who looks but never buys;
And Jones, who seeks for incunabula,
Will spend as much as sixpence any day;
And grumbling Wartface with his hobbling creep
Who churns my tidy stock into a heap.
The whining fingers of the penny mind
Comes picking here, the petty thief, the kind.
And master too, with pot and pipe, who said
He used to deal in rags and never read.
Ah! this is good, my dusty boards grow bare—
A company of quartos go to share
Three sets in ragged calf—dull thoughts on God—
Through which a mind—as dull—will grimly plod.
And now we close; but, in the eventide,
Lie scattered leaves left by a libricide.

IV. THE OLD SOAK

Ah, there he sits, the thirstiest of throats;
Through reveries of beer he drifts and floats.
He has a cadger's grin and muddy eyes:
Sits patiently for fools and free supplies.
In his besotted brain one fact is clear:
His throat's a kiln, is parched, it must get beer.
Some thirty years before he used to work,

Playing with pipes and bricks—these signs still lurk
Upon his grimy rags. This parasite
To pints: this bar and workmate's blight,
Is like a keg: his black-toothed mouth the hole
That long has liquidated mind and soul.

This cheap comedian's hiccoughing clown
Who staggers upon the stage to tumble down—
This mildewed sot revolts the eye and nose.
But when the workhouse walls about him close
A younger drunk will rise, and once again
Within the vacant chair a soak will reign.

V. PARK ORATOR

King of the crowd, outlined against the sky
He brawls denunciations, preens his I.
The masses are his fountains, drinks applause;
Swaggers, defies and rants against the laws.
His supple frog's mouth harshly cataracts
A gush of figures and uncertain facts.
He catches a heckler's jeer, he has a bone;
Something to bite upon, then back it's thrown.
He hurls a grievance, threatens the crowd and air;
With knuckly fist tangles his scanty hair.
He feels colossal; many times the size
To those below who stare with intent eyes.
When walking he is strangely unimpressive,
But here his clichés seem profound and massive:
Knows answers to all sciences, all creeds:
Solves, in a phrase, man's sufferings and needs.
And all these riddles flung from his harsh throat
Lie in a little notebook in his coat.
Another orator, and he steps down:

Talks to a friend, then borrows half-a-crown.
See, there he shuffles off. There's not a bellow
Within this small, deflated, fireless fellow.

VI. THE OLD ACTOR

Dewlapped, in mastiff mold, his mouth orates
Above stained stock, in voice that rants and grates
His battered coins of clichés at the young
Who grin, then later mimic pose and tongue.
An overture of brag roars through his brain
With cataract of encores as refrain.

In retrospect two curtain calls have grown
To ten, the small theatre vast—a throne,
Where memory expands, balloons, uplifts
To magnify his mediocre gifts.
The purple wares of medieval plays
Hue his remembrance, tinsel his mock frays;
The loot from acts, the air a clang of swords,
Stage deaths in sparkling diadems of words;
And debris of his Romeos uprears
In hosed magnificence.

Now Hamlet's fears
Re-echo hollowly; his stage—a tomb
And he a prince of players and of doom.
He was all love, all Lucifer, all king
Strutting in ermine or mad wandering;
And, as for Bottom, nothing could surpass
His unsurpassèd acting as an ass.
Now cushioning conceit upon the past
He claims he was the greatest—now the last.
All, all is microscopic now, and he

End of a rich dramatic dynasty.
Chameleon-character! When death unwinds
The parts you played, and dust from richer minds
Dissolves, a pauper soul will shiveringly stand
Naked in head and heart, empty each hand

VII. PSEUDO IDEALIST

He sees the world in eiderdown:
Harsh thoughts in silk,
Sharp logic softened,
Brigand moods broken:
Growls of hate cushioned in furry words
Till every state is boneless:

No warrior creeds,
No steeds puffing fire;
No taloned hurricanes to scratch the air
But petal-tender days and muted Junes.
He would have earth in feathers,
All summer and sun:
Man meandering in hazy content.

A glut of good
Ebbing to vapid Utopias,
Passivity the parasite
Feeding upon a syrupy state.

IF VISIONS

If visions could be frozen
And folk of Babylon
In ghostly gold and purple
And the gods they gazed upon
Against our eyes illumined,
The roses of our day
Would vanish into vapour;
Our art would burn away.

If visions could be frozen,
Lost Eden's beauty rise
And Pan's frail piping echo
Old faerie rhapsodies,
Our senses would be wedded
To every flower and bird,
The gods of golden ages
Would once again be heard.

BEYOND DEATH

I

Here sorrows fade,
Here all our passions die;
Fears are allayed
Into serenity.
While beauty wreathes
A soft and stately calm,
And gently breathes
A meditative balm.

No cerements
Of doleful Death lie here;
No wan laments
Sob in the dreamer's ear:
For all the woes
That bruise and break and burn
The soul's repose,
Only on Earth sojourn.

With joyous eye
And morning in the mind,
We quiet lie
And watch our dreams unwind.

II

Our hearts would haste,
Our minds would meditate,
Our hands would waste;
Our spirits watch and wait
Rushing, yet still:
Tangled in Time, yet free:

Could we fulfil
Our nobler destiny?
But now we gaze
With clearer mind and high,
Watching the maze
Wherein men live and die:

Whose figures seem
Illusively arrayed;
Shadows who dream
In mirage and in shade;
Shadows who moan
And breathe from heavy breast,
Praying to own
The sweetness of our rest.

ARCHIVES OF SLEEP

When the stars in haloed light
Guide the ships and guard the night,
Secret blossoms of the brain
That had slept, unfurl again.

All the songs once marred and broken,
Here are whole and clearly spoken;
And the engines of the Earth,
Strangling all her mighty girth,
Are unheard and cannot fret
Treasuries inviolate.

Nothing tumbles down the thought
That from filigree is wrought;
Nothing holds the hand and feet
From becoming free and fleet.

Or we meditate, and reap
From the archives of our sleep,
From the avenues of ages,
From our dim ancestral stages
Fantasies that flow or fly
In an unfamiliar sky:

Until, upon the hazy verges
Of the mind, there roll the surges
From an adamantine day
Where our heavy bodies lay.

YOUTH

If youth, who holds the Springtime in his hand
And weaves great garlands for the world, could stand
   In some pale future, gazing at its dust,
He'd weep for death and snap his golden wand.

But youth has veils before his eager eyes,
Each misty hill with vagrant music sighs;
   So he must hurry through a morning world
To meet the ruins of his paradise.

TO A YOUNG DEAD POET

One slim white book-shroud for a tongue now still.
Here, tremulous lines like ecstatic fires
Lit by a girl's kind eyes. A poem of pride—
All hawk and heaven, and thundering words
To scorch a recent tyrant dead as he.
Some thoughts on life: green meteors of spring;
A silver lyric—ashes of an eve
In longing grief. A cry for cavaliers
To loose Romance from the dark woods of Now;
Shouting of trumpets at a close-clenched world:
A golden war in verse against all wrong.

Another page: and here's a glowing ode
With sceptre, orb and crown: the coronation
Of his mind and soul in royal ritual:
L'envoi in a quatrain crystalline.
Then from his crypt of clay he fled,
The chrysalis awake: so, requiem.

EVENING

At evenfall
When fluting feathered throats
Remotely call
Nature's nocturnal notes:
When veiling boughs
To vagrant breezes nod
While gently flowers
The muted light of God,
We who review
Our harvests blown to dust
Again renew
Our faded faith and trust.
The air grows winged
With waking reveries,
And we are ringed
Amid quiet melodies.
Now nothing mars
The hopes our hearts caress;
Linked to our stars
We mould new loveliness.

THE FAILURE

Give him the garland now,
    His finale rite,
And wreathe it round his brow
    Now locked in night.
The songs he sang were small
    And dimly fired,
Yet they were born from all
    His heart inspired.
Give him the spurs and cloak
    He strove to don,
Although he feebly spoke
    And stumbled on.
His visions were too wide,
    His voice too thin;
His verses lacked the pride
    He felt within.
Give him the flowers he grew,
    That would not keep.
Give him their beauty
    To sweeten his sleep.

NUANCES OF SPRING

How lovely this! Spring spilleth everywhere
In delicate beginnings—branches wake
And wintry twigs glint emerald. The spare
Sharp-edged days grow soft; green fabrics make
A tender veil for breezes to caress,
And tight-locked hours, unbarred, no longer press.
We walk with limb-laved lightness—skyward
    tranced,
The caverned thoughts hear singing, haste to leap

The subtle parapets of air. Enhanced
By nuances of spring, the senses sweep,
Expand, embrace with touch of eye and ear
The fragrant freshets of the atmosphere.

THE MATERIALIST

Reaching no rapture of a Christian's hope,
Nor Peri breasts of Islam's paradise,
He holds death in descent: a tangled slop
That stills the sunless fool, the sunlit wise.
Virtue's kind palms gain no celestial gold
Nor Hell binds flames about a rogue's sly wraith;
The haloed act to heaven is not told
And evil splits the good man's rock of faith.

To the dark strong the purple and the throne,
To the wild winds the sobbing of a wood;
The structures of all destinies are blown
With all our tender particles of good.
How else these monumental hurts that press
Upon the fabric of all living things?
And yet compassion burgeons from distress
And, hiddenly, immortal music rings.

SLAVES

The days are steel:
The metal of this age
   That cannot feel,
Has barred us in a cage;
   Where shaft and rod
Plunge through our souls and end
   Our faith in God:
He who we thought a friend.
   Beleaguered by
The wheels that roll and ring,
   We watch the sky
Where birds go fluttering.
   Our minds grow bent
And withered as our lives:
   The instrument
On which the system thrives.
   Thus we who won
Our way through primal sap
   To greet the sun,
Gaze—from a mental trap.

HATHA YOGA

If, like a serpent, you can writhe and wrestle
Until your limbs about your features nestle,
Or raise your haunches till they stare at heaven—
Hoping to wake your *chakras*, one to seven:
Or lie on nails, to prove by some strange twist,
The God you worship is a masochist:
Or try to catch Nirvāna through your navel,
And esoteric mysteries unravel:

If you can twine your limbs about your torso,
Then give another turn, then more and more so,
Till toes and mouth and anus are so mixed
That screams for help are heard, to be unfixed:
If, as an ultimatum to the Powers,
You stand upon your head for many hours,
Look like a spiral, square or pyramid,
A monstrous crab, a cabbage or a squid:
Seek heaven through a complicated pose
Or, squatting, chase *samādhi* through your nose:

Another incarnation might reveal
Existence in the body of an eel.

EVOLUTION

We are all sparks of Him
    Prisoned in earth,
Cast over heaven's brim
    Into black birth
Forgetting the sparks will rise,
    Burning through clod
Up into Paradise,
    Gods greeting God.

Miscellaneous Poems

HERBS

Here Nature's pharmacy in hedge and field
A thousand gentle revelations yield
Without the cost of clinics, doctor's fees;
The via dolorosa of disease.

Through fragrances and colour, leaf and stalk,
Earth's ministries of healing subtly talk;
Nature, who holds in myriad cups of cure
All aids to make the impure body pure.

[*Catalogue and Review* (London: Atlantis Bookshop, 1947), p. 11.]

NOW ALL THE MIND MAJESTICAL

Now all the mind majestical, a star
Cascading light and music from afar;
All of the I translucently arrayed;
All of the me half-glad and half-afraid.
The shouting deeps grow still; the chasms close;
The heights all petalled are in one vast rose;
All radiant the clay; royal the heart;
The eyes—unsealed—behold celestial art.

[*Catalogue and Review* (London: Atlantis Bookshop, 1947), p. 17.]

CHELA'S BOOK OF NURSERY RHYMES

LITTLE CHELA

Little Chela, weak and wavering
    Undecided, here and there;
You will rarely, barely, ever
    Find by using too much care.

Fearful of the steps before you:
    Frightened by the things you heard,
You will never find your Heaven
    When your senses are so blurred.

Little Chela, be decided:
    Use your purpose like a spear,
If you fail to hit the target,
    It might get a little near.

And with greater skill in striking,
    Confidence will enter in
Then your tangled world will vanish
    For another: crystalline.

TEN LITTLE CHELAS

Ten little Chelas
Tried to be Divine

["Little Chela" and "Ten Little Chelas" appeared together in *Catalogue and Review* (London: Atlantis Bookshop, 1947), pp. 25–26; the latter was also published separately as a broadsheet with illustrations by Hugh Deane (London: Atlantis Bookshop, 1947). The untitled poem is found under the heading "From a *Chela's Book of Nursery Rhymes*" in *Occult Observer* (London), vol. 1, no. 4 (1950): p. 245.]

One worked a ritual:
Then there were nine.

Nine little Chelas
Tried to levitate,
One suddenly succeeded:
Then there were eight.

Eight little Chelas
Hammering at Heaven,
One hit the wrong way:
That left seven.

Seven little Chelas
Tried alchemic tricks;
One played with sulphur:
Then there were six.

Six little Chelas
Dark methods did revive;
One left the magic circle:
Then there were five.

Five little Chelas
Went on an occult tour;
One met a Yogi:
This left four.

Four little Chelas
Sat meditatively;
One tried projection:
Then there were three.

Three little Chelas
Worked a witches brew;
One took a sip:
Then there were two.

Two little Chelas
Thought to try a fast;
One overdid it:
That left the last.

One little Chela
Now becoming wise;
Listened to his High Mind:
Earned his Paradise.

[UNTITLED]

Once a chela, eager ninny,
Tried to raise the Kundalini,
Having heard that it would shower
Every kind of magic power.
So he read and practiced breathing
Till he had his centres seething:
Bubbling until overloaded
Cell and nerves and brain exploded.
Fifty volts for a five-watt mind
Nature surely had never designed.

Atomic Journey

A PLAY IN THREE ACTS

CAST OF CHARACTERS

IN THE ORDER OF THEIR APPEARANCE

SIR GIFFARD MACKENZIE

JOSEPH LIMPETT

DR. WILBUR VINE, PH.D., D.SC., M.A.

LADY ESTELLE MACKENZIE

"BILL" SYLVESTER

EUGENE BONSOR

LETTY MOWBRAY

A PRESS PHOTOGRAPHER

BULLIVANT

ANTHONY JEFFRIES

IOLAIR

EALA

MR. SALES MACADAM

DAPHNE

BERNARD HARRINGTON-BERTRAM

A PILOT

A NURSE

TIME—Tomorrow

[London: Michael Houghton, 1954. Co-authored by James J. Eaton]

ACT I

*The managing Director's Room in the London Head
Office of* INTERPLANETARY DEVELOPMENT SERVICES,
LIMITED.

[SIR GIFFARD MACKENZIE *is seated at his desk in his
room—impressively but austerely modern in its office
furnishing—at the London headquarters of* INTER-
PLANETARY DEVELOPMENT SERVICES, LIMITED, *a
public company of recent formation which* SIR GIFFARD
*has established, with himself as Managing Director.
His confidential secretary,* JOSEPH LIMPETT, *is bend-
ing obsequiously over his shoulder; suave in manner,
but fussy under stress,* LIMPETT *is trying, but with
scant success, to gloss over some disputed points in the
draft Prospectus of the Company which lies on the desk
before them.*

SIR GIFFARD, *a big man of powerful physique, ar-
rogant in manner, masterful by habit rather than by
nature, has evidently modelled his mien and bearing
on the late non-lamented Mussolini, whom he slightly
resembles. Now he brings down his fist heavily on the
desk—and taking up the Prospectus with a sharp ges-
ture of disgust, holds it before him as he sits magisteri-
ally in his swivel chair.*]

SIR GIFFARD [*snarls*]. This won't do, Limpett ... won't
do at all! How many years have you been with me
now?

LIMPETT [*nervously*]. Ten, Sir Giffard.

SIR GIFFARD [*raging, contemptuous*]. Ten years! And
you had the effrontery to draft this prospectus as if
INTERPLANETARY DEVELOPMENT SERVICES were

93

a philanthropic institution to finance scientific re-
search. Where's your nous, man? In all this—[*taps
the prospectus*]—where do I come in?

LIMPETT [*fumbles, seeking relevant clause*]. Well, Sir ...
here ... under clause (*c*) ... that very small type, Sir
Giffard ... as Managing Director you draw a salary
of twenty thousand ... and it rises to fifty thousand
when the profits exceed—

SIR GIFFARD [*savagely interrupting*]. So I'm to have fifty
thousand—not even free of tax, out of a ten million
pound share issue! Chickenfeed, Limpett: Do you
think I'm just a ... a ... public benefactor, eh? Lucky
I read the proof before I went, or you would have
left me very nearly a pauper!

LIMPETT [*ingratiatingly*]. Then there's another fifty thou-
sand out of the underwriting, and the ten thousand
for your personal expenses, Sir Giffard.

SIR GIFFARD. Very generous, I'm sure. And dividends
on my Founders' shares limited to one-third of the
profits. Now, get this clear, Limpett. One way and
another, I want a million out of this share issue and
then at least half as much again every year. I don't
care how you fix it, but see that I get it!

LIMPETT [*trying to soothe, but worried*]. Of course, Sir
Giffard ... of course, just as you say. But the new
Act makes it very difficult ... I don't see how....

SIR GIFFARD [*flaring up again*]. You don't see how; what
do I pay you for? If I knew all the financial ins and
outs myself, you would soon lose your job! Have you
forgotten our subsidiary companies? [*His face lights
up, and he almost chuckles.*] By Jove, how the public
will love 'em. [*He recites the names sonorously, showman-
like:*] COSMIC UNIVERSAL COMMUNICATIONS; ASTRO-
GATION ACCESSORIES; STELLAR RAYS LIGHT AND

POWER CORPORATION; LUNAR MINERALS, INC. [*Reverts to hard-boiled, crafty manner:*] Now, Limpett, those companies were made to be milked. And you've got to see to it they are milked, good and proper!

LIMPETT [*with a show of alacrity*]. Very well, Sir Giffard.

SIR GIFFARD [*stands up, leaves his chair, tears the draft Prospectus across with a Napoleonic gesture, and throws the pieces irritably into the wastepaper basket*]. Be off then! Draft the new clauses at once, and get the revise back to the printers by five o'clock. Mmm ... but that means I can't see another proof before we leave.

LIMPETT. Oh ... I could tell them it must be in Macadam's hands tomorrow morning; then he can read it to you over the radio-telephone in the afternoon.

SIR GIFFARD. Ah! that will be the first telephone conversation from space. Make a note of that for the Press, Limpett.

[*LIMPETT receives these instructions with an ingratiating but troubled smile. He takes out a handkerchief and mops his forehead.*]

What's the matter, man? Are you getting scared about the journey?

LIMPETT [*with a rather ghastly smile*]. Scared? N ... no, of course not, Sir Giffard.

SIR GIFFARD [*grunts*]. Well, get along then. Hurry! And on your way out ask Dr. Vine to come in.

LIMPETT. Right, Sir.

[*He hurries out. SIR GIFFARD stands before the fireplace in what he deems a commanding attitude of deep concentration and, when VINE enters a moment later, seems unaware of him for several seconds. Then, with an assumed start ....*]

SIR GIFFARD. Ah, yes, Dr. Vine ... good afternoon.

[*VINE bows, rather coldly.*]

Must we leave at nine tonight? I still have a great deal to do, and there must be no loose ends. You know my passion for perfection ... for precision.

[*Whilst speaking, he has taken and offered cigarettes.* VINE *does not take one, but, placing his gloves and brief-case on the desk, sits down without invitation, then replies. He speaks always with careful deliberation.*]

VINE. We must start at nine o'clock as arranged. Every calculation has been dovetailed to the last second and millimetre ... and that involves the return journey, too. The Moon will not change her orbit for the most eminent financier.

SIR GIFFARD [*a trifle glumly*]. No, no ... hm ... rather awkward, though. I have spent more time than I could spare finding someone to take Jenkin's place —my man, you know. Had him twenty years, but he got cold feet about coming with us. Now fellow, Bullivant ... trifle austere, but seems capable. You're sure we can't make a later start, eh?

VINE. Quite sure.

SIR GIFFARD. Oh, well. Can't be helped ... but very awkward. I did not want to pass the final proof of our prospectus tonight. The share lists open on Wednesday, and all over the country investors will get their prospectuses with their morning papers telling the whole story of our successful flight "on this great cosmic venture"—that's the touch! [*He draws himself up impressively at the thought of his own greatness: then, unbending into a smile, he adds:*] The public will put up ten million pounds for the shares all right. They'll be screaming for more when we get back.

VINE [*not particularly impressed*]. You realise, Sir Giffard, the risks we are taking?

SIR GIFFARD [*brushes this aside*]. Of course, of course . . . but my ventures never fail.

VINE [*continues, unimpressed*]. Ours will be the first interstellar journey ever made by man. Atomic power will give us an incredibly high speed, but we have to travel many thousands of miles, and the cosmos holds many secrets, [*pause*] many perils.

SIR GIFFARD. You made long and elaborate experiments —they cost enough, God knows!

VINE. Yes, but on some points practical tests were impossible. For instance, we could not make a working model of the Moon with our atmosphere to match— so much is conjecture. We have our breathing masks, but will they prove adequate? Can we land at all? We do not know. Our automatic decelerator works perfectly against the gravitational pull of the earth, but some hidden factor may make it useless. And suppose, in the first ten minutes, we accelerate too soon and go too fast, we and our ship will vanish in a flash of instant incandescence.

SIR GIFFARD. Damn it, man, we have gone over all this before! Do you want to drop the whole thing now?

VINE [*coldly*]. Of course not. But you must keep these possibilities in mind.

SIR GIFFARD. The scientific direction of our expedition is in your hands—with myself, of course, as its leader. We need have no fears

[*There is a buzz.* SIR GIFFARD *stops talking, looks at the machine on his desk and says to* VINE, *before pressing the button:*]

Excuse me, Lady Mackenzie on the phone.

[VINE *walks to the window.*]

SIR GIFFARD. Yes, my dear?

LADY MACKENZIE. We have finished your packing. Is all going well with you in the City?

SIR GIFFARD. Yes, of course, Estelle . . . All according to plan. I have Dr. Vine with me now.

LADY MACKENZIE. Oh, I must warn you—Bill's on his way to see you.

SIR GIFFARD [*irritably*]. What does he want?

LADY MACKENZIE. He says he has decided to go with you.

SIR GIFFARD. Come with us! Impossible. Now, Estelle, we had all this out before.

LADY MACKENZIE. Yes, but I still don't understand why you don't want him. After all, he is my brother, so you might be more reasonable about this.

SIR GIFFARD. Don't I know he's your brother. He'll be the ruin of me some day. What is the good of an irresponsible poet on this expedition?

LADY MACKENZIE. He says he will look after you, see that you don't get into any scrapes, and generally brighten the journey.

SIR GIFFARD. Psha! His usual impudence. No, I'm sorry, Estelle, I can't agree.

LADY MACKENZIE. Oh, but you must, Giffard. It seems he has been rather indiscreet; Pamela Gall is threatening to marry him out of hand. Bill says it's go with you, or bust, socially . . . and he says you would hate a scandal.

SIR GIFFARD [*miserably*]. My dear, though he is your brother—[*pause*]—He must have got himself into a hell of a mess. Well, I'll see him . . . but I promise nothing.

LADY MACKENZIE. All right, Giffard. By the way, your new man, Bullivant, seems very efficient. Well, I won't waste any more of your time. Good luck with the rest of your preparations ... and don't be late for dinner—six-thirty. Remember, it will be your last on earth ... until you come back.

SIR GIFFARD. Right, my dear. Good-bye. [*Presses button.*] Damn and blast ... these cursed relations: [*Turning to VINE*] You have not met Bill Sylvester, my wife's brother, have you? One of these damned idealists! Hates me like poison, but he wants to come with us, confound him! I suppose there will be room for him, if I agree?

VINE. Well, there is a certain margin ... I have confirmed young Jeffries' appointment as my assistant on the trip ... but, besides him, the ARGONAUT can still carry one or two more passengers.

[*Opening his briefcase, he takes out a long schedule which he shows to SIR GIFFARD.*]

You see, we have stores in plenty—within, of course, the limits of economy you imposed.

SIR GIFFARD. I always take care of the shareholders' money.

[*Slight pause, during which SIR GIFFARD examines his well-manicured nails. There is a slight tap on the door. A further slight pause. Then a louder but still hesitant tap, and the door half opens to admit first the clerical hat in hand, and then, the head of a large clergyman. With an over-sweetly ingratiating smile the REVEREND EUGENE BONSOR insinuates himself into the room and bows deferentially.*]

BONSOR. Er ... er ... good day, gentlemen. I hope I am not disturbing you. [*He oozes charm.*]

SIR GIFFARD [*glaring*]. Disturbing us? Of course you are. [*Brusquely:*] What do you want?

BONSOR. This letter, Sir ... explains everything.

SIR GIFFARD. Give it to my secretary, Limpett.

BONSOR [*winningly*]. I would prefer you to read it, Sir Giffard.

SIR GIFFARD. Oh, very well. Excuse me, Vine.

[*He takes the letter, reads it, then says, almost cordially:*] So Lord Firth wants me to take you with us, eh? He says you told him that after five years' missionary work in the Hoolitonga Islands you can face anything. But he did not tell you how risky it would be.

BONSOR. I am more than willing to place myself in the hands of Providence—and, of course, your own. [*He bows again.*]

SIR GIFFARD [*turns to VINE, explaining*]. Lord Firth is one of our biggest backers. He's put up two million already. He asks me to take this reverend gentleman. [*Reflecting.*] Do us no harm to have a clergyman aboard . . . Church's blessing on the expedition. Can we manage it . . . eh, Dr. Vine?

VINE [*without enthusiasm*]. Yes, if you wish it.

BONSOR [*coming forward with great bonhomie, clasps SIR GIFFARD's hand in his two hands and shakes it impulsively whilst SIR GIFFARD tries to withdraw it. Breathing heavily and radiating smiles, BONSOR gushes*]. Sir Giffard, you have made me so happy. Now, I shall be able to carry the Lord's work into new fields afar —[*whinnying*] heavenly fields, eh?

SIR GIFFARD [*succeeds in recovering his hand, grunts*]. Well, you can thank the Lord . . . Firth for that. We start tonight at nine o'clock.

BONSOR [*Beams, does a very slight pirouette*]. Oh, yes, I have everything packed—everything. Why, my Dorcas workers have even knitted me a special vest. [*Whinnying again*] and socks, too—long, woolly ones.

SIR GIFFARD. Hm! So you've thought of everything, too.

Very well, Limpett will give you the time, place and full instructions.

[*There is now heard a voice singing in the outer office —a familiar lilting tune, and in a second or two, the door is flung open and* SYLVESTER *strides in, full of joie de vivre. Carefree, he throws his beret on the desk, on the corner of which he sits.*]

SYLVESTER [*breezily*]. Hullo, Mack ... [*stops on seeing* VINE.] Sorry ... didn't know you were engaged.

[*Then he catches sight of* BONSOR, *who stands with one hand behind his back, and his hat in the other hand, beaming at the charts on the wall.*]

Have I burst in on a conference?

SIR GIFFARD [*introducing*]. Oh, Vine ... my brother-in-law, Mr. Sylvester.

[*VINE bows.*]

And this is [*refers to the letter which he is still holding*] the Reverend Eugene Bonsor ... Mr. Sylvester.

BONSOR. A fellow voyager, I hope.

SYLVESTER. Certainly, I'm coming.

SIR GIFFARD. Not so fast, Sylvester! Who said you were coming?

SYLVESTER [*slightly surprised*]. Didn't Estelle phone you?

SIR GIFFARD [*grudgingly*]. Yes, she did. But I told her it's preposterous. This is to be a business trip: We have no room for luxuries. Perhaps you were [*sneeringly*] proposing to recite some of your own verse to us [*laughs unpleasantly*] en route.

SYLVESTER. And why not? [*dramatically*]. Per ardua ad astra.

BONSOR [*interposes*]. Oh, very neat, Sir. And that *is* the way we're going.

SYLVESTER [*receives this rather coldly, and turns to* SIR

GIFFARD]. Now, Mack, it's no use your objecting.
Estelle says I'm coming, and I am.

[*Through the open door the noise of typewriters clack-ing at intervals and other slight office noises can be heard.* LIMPETT *is now seen about to enter, but he is preceded by* LETTY MOWBRAY, *who makes a most ef-fective entrance—perfectly self-assured, for she has no inhibitions, no illusions about rank or money, nor—still less—about men; a radiant, healthy animal, smiling, smoking, swaying at the hips. She walks across to* SIR GIFFARD's *desk and stubs her cigarette in his ash tray.* LIMPETT *follows, a dependent figure in her wake. Her entrance has stopped the conversation dead, and there is a pause. Then* LETTY, *anticipating* SIR GIFFARD's *obvious intention to do some straight talking, breaks in:*]

LETTY. Yes, Sir Giffard, I know exactly what you're going to say ... but please don't say it. I have not forgotten our last interview—

SIR GIFFARD. Interview! I never gave you one.

LETTY. But, Sir Giffard, journalists always come back. At this moment you are Big News, and the *Gazette* expects me to get the low-down on your trip, so here I am!

SIR GIFFARD. My Publicity Man gave the Press every-thing yesterday. I have nothing to add.

LETTY. But, Sir Giffard, *you* were not there. I want your own story ... characteristic, you know, and personal.

SIR GIFFARD [*crisply*]. If I were to give you something personal, you wouldn't like it. [*Emphatically:*] In any case I'm giving no favours to the *Gazette*. It has done its best to ridicule and drag down all my schemes for Empire expansion ... this expedition more than all.

LETTY. Sir Giffard, whatever the *Gazette* has said about

you, I can tell you in confidence that Lord Bilking himself really admires you immensely ... I can't tell you how much.

SIR GIFFARD. He has a queer way of showing it. No, Miss Mowbray, charming as you may be personally, I don't believe you.

[LETTY *is silent for a few seconds, then looks around; her glance falls first on the susceptible* SYLVESTER, *who at once responds with a smile; then she looks meltingly at* BONSOR, *who is still holding and fumbling with his hat, turning it round. He blushes, bows and smirks ... coughs slightly, then shakes his head.* LETTY *again turns to* SYLVESTER, *who answers her unspoken appeal.*]

SYLVESTER. You know, Mack, you may dislike the *Gazette*, but it has a wonderful circulation ... and [*slyly*] some wonderful reporters!

SIR GIFFARD [*ironically*]. Wonderful reporters, yes ... wonderful circulation, yes ... but I'm giving it nothing. That is my last word. Now, Miss Mowbray, I am sure you will understand we are exceedingly busy. We have no time for playful badinage. I wish you good day.

[LETTY *seems to have accepted defeat.* LIMPETT *begins to accompany her to the door, but* SYLVESTER, *all smiles, intercepts him and gets there first. He bows her out .... When she is framed in the doorway she turns and waves her hand, with bag in it, and says lightly:*]

LETTY. Parting is such sweet sorrow! I'll be seeing you.

[*Giving a special smile to* SYLVESTER, *she goes.*]

SIR GIFFARD [*with relief*]. Phew! These women! Thank God, now we can get ahead. Let me see ... I think we have practically finished. Have you anything more to ask me, Vine?

VINE [*after looking at a schedule, which he ticks and then puts down on the desk with a gesture of finality*]. No! I will adjust matters for the two additional passengers.

SIR GIFFARD [*turns to LIMPETT*]. Now Limpett. What about the prospectus?

LIMPETT. Everything is in order, Sir Giffard. I have kept a copy of the revise for you. Here it is.

> [*He hands the paper to SIR GIFFARD, who stuffs it into his breast pocket.*]

SIR GIFFARD. Well, gentlemen, there is just one other matter.

> [*LIMPETT goes to a side table, where there are glasses and drinks, and hands them round.*]

We must drink a stirrup cup. [*Aside to LIMPETT:*] Bring in the photographer.

> [*LIMPETT goes out and brings back a cameraman, who rapidly gets into position. SIR GIFFARD stands in the middle of the stage, with the rest grouped round him, spotlight on him.*]

Here's to the ARGONAUT of the stars! . . . and confusion to Johnson and his crowd of bright lads popping their silly rockets around space like schoolboy crackers. We'll be back before they get started.

> [*There is a flash.*]

BONSOR [*whinnying*]. And may this ARGONAUT bring us back the Golden Fleece!

SYLVESTER [*emphatically*]. Fleece! . . . she will!

> [*Curtain.*]

END OF ACT I

ACT II

SCENE I

The interior cabin of the Atomic spaceship ARGONAUT *en route for the Moon.*

[*The interior cabin of the atomic driven spaceship* ARGONAUT, *shaped like a broad cigar with partly curved convex ceiling and floor, with a fair-sized oblong window placed horizontally in the centre of the back wall. Nearest the window, on its left is the main controls panel, from which are regulated the motive power, and the automatic of the window carries the working keys for wireless communications, heating, lighting, air conditioning and oxygenation pilot device. A rather similar panel set on the other side and the operation of all doors, including that into the airlock.*

Immediately adjacent to, level with and within easy reach of, the main controls panel, is the pilot's bunk, and on this same side there are three other bunks, the four being ranged in two tiers, the lower pair about two feet from the floor, and beyond these, with its base on the floor, is a big upright stores locker with a narrow fanlight, open at the top. On the right hand side of the central window are four more bunks arranged in two tiers, but with another upright locker between them. The cabin has three doors. Lighting is by means of neon tubes flush with the ceiling and walls, but the two red emergency lights are of the ordinary type of pendant bowls fitted close to the ceiling. Seven chairs, grouped round a table, all clamped to the floor, occupy a recess to the right, only a short distance from the airlock chamber which gives egress from the vessel. There are hand-holds on the walls, floor and ceiling of

105

the cabin. Near the centre of the stage is a long plain divan.

When the curtain rises there seems to be no one on the stage: the whole of the interior cabin is shuddering violently and there is a dull rushing noise. The interior lighting is dimmed until the ARGONAUT *passes out of the Earth's atmosphere. A slight pause, then* VINE *is seen to raise himself to a sitting position in his bunk, over the side of which is extended his right hand, holding an electric torch, whose light he directs upon the main controls panel above, so that he takes a reading from the panel into a small circular mirror inclined, at eye-level, at a suitable angle towards him. His face, tense with strain, is bathed with sweat.*]

VINE [*huskily, just audible*]. Speed is right, acceleration exact. We have been in flight six minutes already; in less than two minutes more we shall be clear of the stratosphere, and the pressure will be eased.

LIMPETT [*prone in his bunk, cries half muffled, whimpers*]. I can't stand it! [*gasping*] It's killing me!

VINE [*comforting, but sounds slightly annoyed*]. Lie perfectly still, man, and you will be all right.

SYLVESTER [*also lying prone, raises his hands to speak*]. We can take it: we've no option.

LIMPETT [*groans*]. My God, it's awful.

[VINE *continues to take his readings by inspection of the mirror. After a few moments the shuddering movements and noise cease, and all is still and silent.*]

VINE [*evidently relieved*]. We are out of the stratosphere: You can relax; but take it gently. Don't attempt to get up.

[VINE'*s hands are fingering at the control board and his head is again just visible above the side of his bunk.*

A silent purring murmur is now audible throughout this scene.]

Now that we are running on atomic power, our speed is [*slowly*] almost exactly nine miles per second.

[*From the outer banks, heads are poked out in irregular succession. Now a voice breaks in on the loudspeaker:*]

VOICE. This is x2 calling the ARGONAUT ... x2 calling the ARGONAUT.

VINE [*presses button, then speaks into the microphone*]. This is the ARGONAUT, Wilbur Vine speaking.

VOICE. Good luck, ARGONAUT: Keep in touch.

SYLVESTER [*pokes his head over the side of his bunk, speaking wearily, but trying to sound bright*]. Who is x2, Vine?

VINE. x2 is the Mount Everest-peak station.

SYLVESTER. Jolly good: Can we get up now?

VINE. No. You are all exhausted and must sleep. I will keep watch.

[*The curtain is dropped to indicate a lapse of time. When it rises, VINE is out of his bunk and stands examining a pressure dial on the second control panel. Then he scrutinizes the large luminous chart screen—a sheet of deep blue glass on which the vessel's course is shown by a clear yellow moving line (use neon light). At present the line is practically horizontal and as straight as a ruler. VINE calls loudly:*]

You can all leave your bunks now, if you like; but see that you have your magnetic boots on.

[*As they emerge, it is seen that all are wearing clothing of a strictly functional kind, of leather, close fitting with some metal gadgets, and leather helmets. Only VINE wears a special contraption in his helmet. SIR GIFFARD, the first to appear, seems less assured than his usual carefully groomed, Savile-Row tailored, City*] *self. Perhaps he misses the daily carnation from his buttonhole. Certainly he hates wearing this odd, space-travel suit identical with that of each of his fellow astronauts, for it robs him of distinction, so that he looks more like a commonplace engineering hand in overalls than a mighty financier and captain of industry. Conscious of this, he stands very stiffly, silent, then fumbles among strange pockets for cigar case and matches. His cigar lighted, his bearing at once becomes rather more masterful and he goes over to VINE.]*

SIR GIFFARD. Well, what's your report, Vine?

[They go aside to confer. By now all the rest of the party, except BONSOR and JEFFRIES, are loosely grouped near the centre of the stage and begin to talk.]

LIMPETT. That awful first five minutes: I was pounded to a pulp.

SYLVESTER. Why, man, we had only just begun. Where's your imagination? Think of where you are now: A speck of Infinity, sitting on nothing.

[LIMPETT shudders, groans again and climbs back into his bunk. BULLIVANT, silent and apparently unperturbed, proceeds to take from the locker on the left some gadgets for refreshments, screwing each covered glass and plate to the table with a deft swiftness that makes the operation seem as natural to him as if he had been doing it all his life.]

BONSOR *[is now seen peering shortsightedly over the side of his bunk]*. Oh, Dr. Vine, Dear, dear, me, is it quite safe now? What an experience: We have been most mercifully preserved.

SYLVESTER *[mischievously]*. Did you pray, Mr. Bonsor?

BONSOR *[bleats]*. Alas, no! I was ... hm, slightly unwell ... and then unconscious.

[*He peers about in the depths of his bunk, using a torch, then brings up his hat, his umbrella and his hymn book, all of which he clutches tightly. He climbs down gingerly via the bunk below and goes to stand beside* VINE, SIR GIFFARD *and* SYLVESTER, *who are now looking out of the window into the blackness of space. A white trail of meteors flashes past, then beyond the window all is deep black again. Then* SYLVESTER *breaks the silence:*]

SYLVESTER. My God. The immensity ... and that distant little ball down there ... I suppose that's the Earth, eh, Vine?

VINE. Yes.

SYLVESTER. How dare we ... we insects ... break into this infinity of space!

SIR GIFFARD [*smugly*]. It's damn remarkable. But you poet fellers talk a lot of poppycock about voyaging the heavens. There's nothing mystical about space navigation. Finance, you know ... and [*patronisingly*] science, can do anything. *I* had no doubts ....

SYLVESTER. Ugh! We are a long way from the Stock Exchange, but not far enough, it seems.

BONSOR. I am beginning to feel a little better. And in this brave company [*he beams round benignly*] loneliness soon passes away. [*Having stressed the last phrase, he remembers cemeterial implications, and adds, hastily:*] Hm ... hm ... no, I mean ... melts ... an insubstantial shadow, you know.

SYLVESTER. Well, I don't feel at home yet among these sister worlds, the asteroids. But how lovely they are .... If I could only sing their splendour:

[*Pausing to turn and take a cigarette from* BULLI-VANT, *he lowers the emotional temperature by a casual question.*]

109

By the way, Bullivant, *you* seem quite at home—a seasoned astronaut. You're not going to tell me you haven't done this trip before!

BULLIVANT [*woodenly*]. Oh, no, Sir.

[*He then proceeds to distribute cigarettes and/or chocolates from special boxes with closed tops into which each has to put his hand to get one. There is heard a dull thud, as of some heavy object striking the hull of the spaceship. LIMPETT, who is just creeping out of his bunk at the time, rushes to the tray for drinks on the table, is about to siphon some soda into a glass but thinks better of it, and, instead, with shaking hands siphons a generous allowance of neat whiskey into a covered glass and drinks it through a straw. VINE, turning away from the window, comes to the centre and addresses them quietly.*]

VINE. There is no cause for alarm . . . . Just a fragment of meteorite grazed the hull. It would have to be much bigger and a direct hit to do any damage. This cabin, a casket suspended on roller-bearing pivots, is cushioned in a vacuum, and insulated against still harder knocks.

[*His hearers have evidently been badly scared, but now show some signs of returning equanimity. VINE looking round, calls:*]

Jeffries! Where is he?

BULLIVANT. He is still in his bunk, Sir.

VINE. That's odd.

[*He strides across to JEFFRIES's bunk, pulls the curtain aside, looks in and calls quietly, "Jeffries." There is no reply. He leans over into the bunk, shakes the young man without result, then brings out JEFFRIES's hand to test the pulse, afterwards letting the hand hang limply over the side of the bunk.*

VINE, perturbed, beckons to BULLIVANT, *who crosses over to the bunk. Between them they lift the unconscious* JEFFRIES *and deposit him on the only settee, a little to the left of centre.* BULLIVANT *goes to his cupboard, from which he brings restoratives, and forces some brandy between* JEFFRIES's *closed lips, whilst* VINE *chafes his hands, etc.* BONSOR, SYLVESTER, SIR GIFFARD *and* LIMPETT, *who have all gathered round to watch, are talking among themselves. After an appreciable pause:*]

BULLIVANT. He's coming round now.

[*The young man is, in fact, showing signs of returning consciousness. He is making incoherent sounds, vaguely muttering to himself.*]

VINE. Are you feeling better now, Jeffries?

[JEFFRIES *does not reply, but nods his head, weakly.*]

What's the matter with you?

[JEFFRIES *shakes his head, tries to speak, mutters something and shudders.* VINE *has glanced across at the control board, now shows some slight impatience:*]

Come, pull yourself together, boy. What is wrong?

JEFFRIES [*in a weak voice*]. Sorry, Sir. The pressure was terrific ... and then that awful smash. I went right out.

VINE [*a hint of contempt in his voice*]. That awful smash, as you call it, was only a meteorite grazing our hull ... a very minor mishap. Are you better now?

JEFFRIES [*rather louder*]. Yes, Sir, I think so.

[*He stands up, but very shakily ... a well-built, not bad-looking young man of strong physique. He turns towards the window, then, swaying as he stands, goes rather white, and averts his head.*]

VINE [*not unkindly*]. Well, you had better sit down again. Take it easy for a time. I shall need your help later.

JEFFRIES. Thank you.

[*He sits down again on the settee.* VINE *turns and addresses the group.*]

VINE. You know, I think this is a good opportunity to tell you a few things about what this machine is doing and what we hope it will do. Just come over and look at the controls panel. It's all very simple.

[*All, except* SYLVESTER *and the drooping* JEFFRIES *on the settee, gather round* VINE *while he demonstrates, rather in the lecturer's manner. Meanwhile,* SYLVESTER *looks sympathetically at the forlorn* JEFFRIES, *slips across to him and, taking a large flask from a capacious side-pocket, hands it to him.*]

SYLVESTER. Take this, young fellow. It will buck you up. There's plenty ... but it's strong.

JEFFRIES [*eagerly, almost snatches the flask*]. Thanks.

[*He takes a long swig. And for the next quarter of an hour or so he is seen to be taking further and frequent, substantial swigs from the flask, and gradually becoming less inert and more restless. How and to what extent he should show, whilst still sitting there, the signs of incipient and growing intoxication, are points for the producer's attention.* SYLVESTER, *as soon as he has handed over the flask, goes across and joins the group, to whom* VINE *is saying:*]

VINE. Now on this small lever depends our keeping our course dead true. That lever is not to be moved at all until we come within a certain closely calculated distance from the Moon.

[*The rest of the group stand listening without movement.* BONSOR *takes out his glasses, rubs them carefully with his handkerchief and puts them on, then pushes his clerical hat with hand back on his head and bends down to peer closely at the lever on which so much depends. Seeing him put a finger out as if to touch it,* SYLVESTER *leans forward and grabs his hand away.*]

SYLVESTER [*conversationally*]. If you play with that lever, Bonsor, we shall get to the Kingdom of Heaven sooner than we need.

BONSOR [*rubs the offending hand as if* SYLVESTER *had bitten it; ruefully*]. He ... he ... you will have your little joke, Mr. Sylvester. I was not going to touch that lever really. And as for getting to Heaven, no one can never get there too soon .... Oh, Mr. Sylvester, you do know that!

SYLVESTER. You need to be sure of your welcome. Because you have a pass, you forget the rest of us are hardened sinners.

[*Suddenly he sniffs, and looks suspiciously at* BONSOR]. Really, really.

BONSOR. What's the matter?

SYLVESTER. Oh, nothing. But I didn't know clergy men used the snuff.

BONSOR [*holding up a waggish forefinger*]. You know, Mr. Sylvester, you are a one!

[*Any further fatuous, maiden-auntly comment from* BONSOR *is prevented by* VINE *addressing them all.*]

VINE [*sternly*]. What Sylvester said lightly, I must emphasise seriously. No one—do you all understand? —NO ONE but myself must touch any of the controls, especially that pilot lever. And so long as I am in charge of this vessel, you will all please do as I say.

SIR GIFFARD [*comes forward into centre, all his feathers bristling*]. You forget yourself, Vine. I, sir, am in command of the ARGONAUT, and no one ... [*he becomes empurpled*] no one, sir, shall give me orders.

VINE. So far as piloting of this ship is concerned, Sir

Giffard, I am the superior officer and expect even you to obey me.

[*He turns, and moves away to the other side of the window.*]

SIR GIFFARD [*almost foaming with wounded vanity*]. By God, Sir, I'll ....

[*Ostentatiously* VINE *pays him no attention, but quietly proceeds to show* BONSOR *and* SYLVESTER *the workings of the minor control-panel from which are manipulated the air conditioning and other necessary services.* SIR GIFFARD *stands, frustrated, in silent rage. To cover his confusion, he beckons to* LIMPETT, *and snarls:*]

Your notebook, man! We must get on with the log. Are you ready?

LIMPETT [*obsequious as ever*]. Yes, of course, Sir Giffard.

SIR GIFFARD. Right! Take this.

[*Consulting some notes taken from his pocket, he begins to dictate, but at first with a slightly feverish emphasis, not quite his usual arrogant self.*]

August 13. In the spaceship ARGONAUT. This is the logbook of the first interstellar traveller, Sir Giffard Mackenzie, in sole command of the expedition.

[*He breaks off suddenly, and says to* LIMPETT:]

See here ... I should be broadcasting this. Everybody, all over the world, will want to hear me. Are we tuned in to Earth?

[LIMPETT *looks at* VINE, *who is still standing by, watching.* VINE *says nothing, but goes to the minor control-panel, twists a knob, then speaks into the microphone.*]

VINE. This is the spaceship ARGONAUT calling. Can you hear us X2? ... ARGONAUT calling X2.

VOICE. This is X2 calling. Go ahead, ARGONAUT. We can hear you quite clearly.

[*Without speaking* VINE *beckons to* LIMPETT, *who goes to the microphone.*]

LIMPETT. Sir Giffard Mackenzie will speak. Please radiate his message to all stations.

[*There is some clicking and buzzing, then—*]

VOICE. Right. X2 here. All stations ready now for Sir Giffard Mackenzie's message.

[SIR GIFFARD *moves slowly to the microphone, an illustrious world figure, stands proudly erect in the spotlight. He has almost forgotten the recent incident, and as he speaks his voice soon reverts to the normal, booming on.*]

SIR GIFFARD. Ha ... hum. [*He repeats:*] This is the logbook of the first interstellar traveller, Sir Giffard Mackenzie, in sole command of the expedition. [*Then proceeds:*] We are voyaging through the vastness of space, en route for the Moon. How soon we may reach there has yet to be proved, for our tests of atomic speeds on earth could give no certain clue to the incredible pace we are making, free from gravitational and atmospheric checks. All goes smoothly here aboard the ARGONAUT. A moment ago, a large meteorite struck our hull, but that was of no consequence. Impervious to cosmic assaults we GO ON! Our task is to emancipate space-bound humanity. WE SHALL DO IT!—and do it with profit, not to our shareholders only, but [*his voice rising on a reverent rallentando, he gives out the final words like a trumpet call*] to MANKIND.

[SIR GIFFARD *stops, takes a deep draught of water. In the brief ensuing pause,* VINE *has halted in front of the locker on the right. Standing beside him,* BONSOR *and* SYLVESTER *await further demonstrations.*]

VINE. This locker holds all the rest of our equipment and accessories, including the atmospheric masks.

[*He pulls the locker door, and out tumbles, with a great clatter, a miscellany of objects, among which are several buckets, all the atmospheric masks and other gadgets. In the midst of all is disclosed the slightly dishevelled, but still attractive, figure of a girl stowaway. BONSOR, SYLVESTER and VINE gather round her, astonished; even BULLIVANT moves a few paces forward to see what she is like, whilst the girl lies sprawled at full length. It is worth noting that she also is wearing a pair of magnetic boots. SYLVESTER steps forward and picks her up. She clings to him closely until he sets her on her feet.*]

SYLVESTER [*amazed in recognition*]. Well! Miss Mowbray!

LETTY. Yes, here I am . . . as I promised.

[*She stretches, yawns, dusts herself down, daintily, with the smallest of handkerchiefs, then takes out a pocket mirror for a quick glance*]

. . . but oh, dear, that was dreadful!

[*Completely at ease, she looks defiantly at SIR GIFFARD, who has moved towards the group. He is evidently furious, sufficiently so to make no attempt politely to conceal it.*]

SIR GIFFARD [*apoplectically*]. My God! You impudent b . . . b . . . baggage! The audacity . . . the, er . . . the cheek of you . . . flaunting my express orders!

[*Words fail him. Before LETTY can reply BONSOR butts in.*]

BONSOR. You know, Miss Letty you have been [*he wags an admonitory forefinger at her*] a very naughty girl . . . very naughty indeed. You might have hurt yourself . . . then what should we have done?

LETTY [*cheekily*]. Kissed the place to make it well. But I have more bruises than I can possibly show you, and I was nearly suffocated in that damned locker.

116

[*Looks into her handbag.*] Blast! My compact's broken and all my powder's gone! Will someone stop gaping and show me to the LADIES, please?

[*The request catches them all unready, except BUL-LIVANT, who goes to one of the doors and opening it, stands aside. As LETTY sweeps past him, he bends respectfully and says a few words quietly; in response, she taps him lightly on the forearm and, with a smile, passes out of sight.*]

SYLVESTER [*to BONSOR*]. I must apologise. When I smelt that face powder earlier one, and couldn't see any, I suspected you.

BONSOR. Oh, Mr. Sylvester ... you have no respect for my cloth!

[*Meanwhile VINE has been examining closely and with evident anxiety the jumble of atmospheric masks, etc. He rises to his feet, and taking SIR GIFFARD aside, speaks to him quietly so that the others shall not hear.*]

VINE. All our parachutes are intact—but this is most serious, Sir Giffard—five out of our six atmosphere masks are damaged beyond repair.

SIR GIFFARD [*haughtily*]. Have we no spares?

VINE. No. You may remember, you complained of the cost, and it was one of your ideas to save expense. Those false economies may wreck everything.

SIR GIFFARD [*hotly*]. It's that cursed girl's fault!

[*Now LETTY returns, radiant. BONSOR stands around, looking sheepish. LIMPETT has edged up to LETTY and under pretext of sympathetic inquiry about her bruises, offers some familiar touches. LETTY, though ready enough to encourage that sort of thing when occasion offers, has yet an eye to the approaching SYLVESTER, so gives a faint squeak when LIMPETT tries to paw her.*]

SYLVESTER [*brushes LIMPETT aside*]. Well, Miss Mowbray,

I admire your daring. You have created a new record ... the first stellar stowaway ... and in spite of Sir Giffard, too. You deserve ... well, something better than he would give you [*gives her an affectionate pat on the shoulder*].

LETTY [*preening herself, winks knowingly*]. STELLAR STOW-AWAY! ... I like that. What do *you* think I deserve, then?

SYLVESTER. Fame, but you will have that anyway. You shall be immortalised ... in lovely verse!

[*He offers her a cigarette, which she takes and he lights.*]

LETTY [*prettily*]. Thank you, Mr. Poet. But I shall want your help as well ... your active help ... to get the biggest scoop ever.

SYLVESTER [*eagerly*]. You may count on me. But what will it be?

LETTY [*non-committal*]. Ah! you shall see!

[BONSOR, *who has been hovering around, now sidles into their company. Whilst* LETTY *is lighting her cigarette he approaches her with studied grace, hat in hand.*]

BONSOR. Miss Mowbray, they tell me you wrote for the *Gazette*, so we are almost colleagues. I am a humble fellow-contributor to the *Gazette*. Last summer they took an article of mine, "Can We Tame Our Wasps?" and then a month ago, I did a slight article on Birds—

SYLVESTER [*guffaws*]. Cheeps from a Rectory garden, eh?

LETTY. He's only envious, Mr. Bonsor. I am sure your articles were very exciting ... and instructive.

BONSOR [*delighted*]. Well, my dear, I did my little best ... just a humble worker in the vineyard.

SYLVESTER [*his lip curls*]. BONSOR the Beloved—the Wasp without a sting!

[*Seeing* BULLIVANT *carrying round a tray of tea,* BONSOR *rapidly does the gallant and offers* LETTY *one, which she takes with a pretty show of thanks. Then, waving them a gay gesture, cup in hand, she trips across gracefully to where* SIR GIFFARD *stands moodily looking out of the window. She touches his arm timidly; he turns abruptly.*]

SIR GIFFARD [*brusque as before, but speaks slowly and tensely*]. What ... do you ... want ... now?

LETTY [*apparently repentant*]. Sir Giffard, I am truly sorry I have offended you. You must find it hard to forgive me.

SIR GIFFARD. Not hard, Miss Mowbray.... Impossible.

LETTY. But, Sir Giffard [*limpidly*] please! This is such a tremendous moment for me. Here I am talking to you—the man for news of whom the whole world is waiting ...the man who *is* news ... the great man of this age.

SIR GIFFARD [*relaxes slightly, somewhat mollified*]. Thank you, young lady. I know. I am attending to all that *personally*.

LETTY. But everyone on Earth wants to know everything about you; what you are like and what you are doing. Oh, Sir Giffard, I promised my Editor.

SIR GIFFARD [*annoyed again; she has touched a sore point*]. Your Editor! I dislike your Editor and your paper. I dislike your Proprietor, his politics, his principles— if he has any, which I very much doubt.

[*He begins to stamp about angrily.*]

He vilifies my work; he misrepresents my aims; he has no vision and no scruples—

SYLVESTER [*butting in*]. In short, my dear, Sir Giffard [*gently*] dislikes your paper.

SIR GIFFARD [*fuming*]. Tcha!

[*He turns on his heel and leaves them.*]

LETTY [*now bringing all her feminine armoury to bear upon sylvester, looks at him, dewy-eyed, with a slight sigh and wiping her eyes with a dainty handkerchief*]. Oh, dear, Mr. Sylvester, what *shall* I do? I must ... I simply must ... radio my paper.

SYLVESTER. But what can you say? Sir Giffard has told them nothing ... nothing fit to print. You have upset him, you know ...by Jove, you have!

LETTY [*piteously*]. Yes, I am afraid so. [*Then defiantly:*] Well, if he won't play, I must. I can use my imagination. Will you help me?

[*She touches his arm, pleadingly, and looks into his eyes.*]

SYLVESTER [*succumbs*]. Of course, my dear girl. What do you want me to do?

LETTY [*half whispers, finger on lips*]. Stand by me while I radio my Editor.

[*And without further she steals across, conspiratorially, to the microphone, unhooks a gadget, waits for a moment or two, then says:*]

This is Letty Mowbray on the spaceship ARGONAUT. Is that the World Central Radio Station?

VOICE. This is x2 speaking? Who do you say you are?

LETTY. I am LETTY MOWBRAY on the spaceship ARGONAUT. Have you got that?

VOICE. Wait a moment, please. [*Pause.*] We have no record on our list of any woman on the ARGONAUT. What are your credentials?

LETTY. Oh, bother: I was a stowaway, if you must know ... but it's quite all right. I want to speak to my paper ... the *Gazette*, London. Please put me through. The number is CENTRAL oof oof oof.

VOICE [*severely*]. Very well, we will put you through, but

if you prove to be hoaxing us—or the *Gazette*—that will be a serious offence.

[*At this moment* VINE *has come along and sees what* LETTY *is doing. He pushes* SYLVESTER *aside and almost rudely snatches the microphone from* LETTY.]

VINE. You must not use the radio without my permission. [*Speaks into the microphone:*] Is that x2?

VOICE. x2 here.

VINE. This is Wilbur Vine, of the ARGONAUT. Please cancel that call.

VOICE. Very well, Dr. Vine. The call is cancelled.

[VINE *replaces the microphone on the hook.*]

LETTY [*livid with disappointment; she has been so near her world-scoop*]. You interfering bastard, you've spoiled everything!

[*At this moment* JEFFRIES, *whose repeated applications to the flask have brought him to a critical point of intoxication, staggers to his feet, waving the flask above his head. He is obviously drunk, but, with an effort, pulls himself together momentarily: then, with a sudden lurch forward, he launches himself into the centre of the stage, wags an admonitory forefinger at* LETTY *and says, thickly—*]

JEFFRIES. Phew! [*hiccoughs*] Language, lady, language.

LETTY. You watch your step, my lad. Impudence!

JEFFRIES [*looks at her admiringly*]. Ra—watch yours, buteful lady . . . .

[*He leers at her.* SIR GIFFARD *and* LIMPETT *are now sitting on the settee, with the notebook in action.* BULLIVANT *is audibly busy in his galley.* BONSOR *and* SYLVESTER *are standing side by side at the nearby window watching asteroids in flight, and are exchanging dramatic gestures. They now half turn to see what's happening with* JEFFRIES, *whom* VINE *is observing closely from nearby.*]

JEFFRIES [*waves the flask again, then offers it to* LETTY].
Have a drink, m'dear. I'm ver' mis'ble. Dishap [*hic*]
pointed. When I was a boy, nose punched, shaw
shtars . . . Dr. Vine promised take me shtars. But no
fim shtars . . . . You fim shtar?

[LETTY *does not reply, shrugs her contempt.* JEFFRIES
piqued, takes another swig:]
Tha's good . . . that's very good!

[*With sudden change of mood, he becomes hilarious
and bursts into song, but in maudlin, dirge-like voice.*]
Wash'll we do with er drunken shailor [*twice repeated,
interspersed with hiccoughs*]. I'm no' drunk, but I'm
shailor. Yesh, schience shailor [*raises his voice*] spaysh.
Don'sh you b'leeve me? 'll show you. [*Roars.*] Know
how work ship. You wash me.

[JEFFRIES'*s bellow has brought* BULLIVANT *post-haste
from his galley. Everyone has stopped talking and is
giving concentrated attention to* JEFFRIES, *who begins
drunkenly to lurch towards the control panel.* VINE
moves swiftly forward to intercept him.]

VINE. What are you up to, Jeffries?

JEFFRIES [*stops, stares at him glassily, swaying*]. Up to?
Going steer ship shtars, course.

VINE [*moving closer to him, raps out*]. Stop where you are!

JEFFRIES [*takes another swig, stares more glassily*]. Can't
shtop now. Busy takin' charge ship. Out my way!

[*He sweeps* VINE *aside, but* VINE *clutches at him as
he moves towards the control panel.* JEFFRIES *eludes
capture, turns, raises flask high and brings it down
on* VINE'*s head—a heavy blow.* VINE *crumples and
falls stunned. Commotion.* SIR GIFFARD *is fussing*

around the circumference of the fray, urging the re-luctant LIMPETT *to* "Grab the feller!" *whilst* LETTY, *withdrawn slightly from the storm-centre, watches keenly.* SYLVESTER *and* BONSOR, *with* BULLIVANT, *rush forward and grab* JEFFRIES *as he reaches the control panel. He stands back to beat them off, and half turns, but his elbow—unseen by them—knocks the pilot-lever which gives a half turn. There is a brief, hiss-ing noise; for a second or two the low purring which is the background sound of the flight is interrupted, then the shutter to the centre window slowly descends and clicks fast, whilst the straight, yellow line on the blue glass of the big illuminated chart of the course de-scribes a swift, jagged trajectory, then swings rapidly back to a straight line again. At once the low purring is resumed. With a hoarse cry* JEFFRIES *shakes off his captors, rushes across the stage, throws open a door and, as they are about to close upon him, disappears and bangs it behind him. His pursuers let him go and gather round the unconscious form of* VINE *still lying on the floor.* BULLIVANT, *who is busy over him, turns to* SYLVESTOR.]

BULLIVANT. He's not badly hurt.

SYLVESTER. Good! Let's make him comfortable on here. [*They lift him on the settee, and* BULLIVANT *continues his ministrations, whilst the rest note the signs of his returning consciousness.*]

SIR GIFFARD. That was a murderous young ruffian ... and disgustingly drunk ... dangerous! Better go after him, Limpett ... see he does no more mischief.

LIMPETT [*evasively*]. He went in there [*pointing to the door*]. He may be waiting to attack anyone who goes after him.

SIR GIFFARD. Well, try the door, and see.

[LIMPETT, *far from eager but not daring to refuse, is moving gingerly towards the door, when* LETTY *forestalls him.*]

LETTY. I'll tackle him. He won't hurt me, drunk as he is, I'm sure. [*She goes to the door, throws it open, and calls through.*] Come along, Mr. Jeffires. Don't stay there sulking. Nobody's going to hurt you.

[*There is no reply.* LETTY *goes forward, past the open door; in a couple of seconds she is out again.*]

What's happened. He's gone.

LIMPETT [*now full of courage, joins her in the doorway*]. Can't be ... nowhere for him to go. Room's no bigger than a cupboard. Is he behind that curtain?

BULLIVANT [*who has now joined them*]. That's not a curtain. That covers the porthole. If he dashed in an dived through there ....

[VINE, *looking pale and shaky, and with his head bandaged, comes forward very slowly to join them. He repeats* BULLIVANT'*s words.*]

VINE. If he dived through there ... he will have been sucked out through the valve into space.

SYLVESTER. And what then?

VINE [*sombrely*]. He wore no spacesuit. He is beyond our help. His body, cushioned upon frictionless space, floats beside us on our journey through the void. But the lad is dead!

*   *   *   *   *

SCENE II

The same as before—but later.

[*Before the curtain rises, the voice of* VINE *is heard saying,* "Now you all know" *and as the curtain rises he finishes the sentence ...* "what we must do."

124

All the members of the ARGONAUT *party are discovered seated, apparently in conference, with* VINE *addressing them. He looks white and drawn, with head still bandaged; the attention of the rest, in serious mood, is concentrated on him. But, as usual,* SYLVESTER'S *expression is slightly quizzical:* LETTY *is watchfully alert ....*]

VINE. ... what we must do.

SIR GIFFARD. I don't like this blind flying, Vine. Can't we force that window shutter somehow?

VINE. No. We wasted an hour trying: nothing will budge it.

SIR GIFFARD. But how can we land safely, when we can't see where we are going?

VINE. Radar is our eye. We may be landing any time now. Our fenders are out, and we are running on momentum only. If the decelerator is working as it should ....

SYLVESTER. If ... don't you know? It's an automatic device, isn't it?

VINE. Yes, but we don't know exactly the gravitational pull of the Moon.

SYLVESTER. So ... it's a toss-up whether we don't land at all, or get an almighty bump?

VINE. We *may* land quite smoothly.

LIMPETT [*panicky*]. Suppose we drop into a crater?

VINE. Whatever happens, there will be problems ... we must be ready to improvise.

SIR GIFFARD [*sneering*]. Improvise ... after all our pre-planning.

BONSOR [*beaming*]. Men and mice, Sir Giffard, men and mice ... we must trust in the Lord.

VINE. We shall test the astronomers' theories and establish the facts.

LETTY. Let's hope those theories are fairy-tales. No atmosphere on the Moon ... that may be wrong. And perhaps we shall not go prancing about like ... like air balloons. Me, I'm all for surprises.

VINE. One French astronomer proved there must be air on the Moon. Later research, however ... Well, we shall know soon ... and about lunar gravity, too.

SYLVESTER. Hurrah for the fantasies of science! But [*slyly*] Miss Mowbray, at least you must be hoping to find the Man in the Moon?

LETTY [*with a cryptic smile*]. That will depend ....

SIR GIFFARD [*abruptly*]. This is no time for fooling. I must say, Vine, our present situation is hardly creditable to ... hum, ha ... yourself.

VINE [*coldly*]. Indeed, Sir Giffard. Why?

SIR GIFFARD. You engaged that young ruffian, Jeffries ....

SYLVESTER [*shocked*]. You are disgusting, Mack! Poor young fellow [*he shudders and points to the shuttered window*] ... drifting out there in that terrible empty darkness ... [*he buries his face in his hands.*]

SIR GIFFARD [*contemptuous*]. Bah! Sentimental drivel! Facts are facts. The cowardly, drunken young scamp might have wrecked the whole expedition.

VINE. He was a young man of great promise ... had studied planetary atmospherics. That justified my choice.

SIR GIFFARD. Did he do a single useful thing for us on the trip?

VINE. No one could foresee the stress that unbalanced him. He was too highly strung.

SIR GIFFARD [*jeering*]. Nothing fragile about him. He knocked you out.

VINE. I bear him no ill-will. Had he lived, he would have gone far.

SIR GIFFARD [*with a nasty laugh*]. He's done that all right, anyway.

[*The faces of all the listening group, except* LIMPETT, *show nauseated surprise and horror at* SIR GIFFARD'*s callous quip.*

There is a silent pause. Then the lights suddenly flicker and go out. The emergency lights do not come on yet. There is a splintering bump and a harsh grating sound. In the darkness is heard a medley of noises, footsteps hurrying to and fro, voices in confusion and alarm. SIR GIFFARD *bellows:*]

What *has* happened?

[*He switches on his torch, revealing the scared faces of the huddled group. At the same moment* VINE *goes to the appropriate panel and switches on the emergency lighting, which burns with a dull, red glow, adding a further touch of strangeness to the scene.*]

VINE [*authoritatively*]. Keep calm, all. There is no immediate danger. No one is injured. The ARGONAUT is damaged—how badly, I cannot say.

SIR GIFFARD. But what is all this? Where are we?

VINE. We have grounded [*pause*]. Some of the instruments—including the radio—are out of action, for the time being at least.

SYLVESTER [*brightly*]. Well, the Moon is not so far from home, after all!

VINE [*ironically*]. No: rather less than two hundred and forty thousand miles. What must be done now is to test if we can get out of the ship. There is only one atmospheric mask undamaged, so you will all have to wait here patiently whilst I make the attempt. I will come back and report as quickly as possible.

[*In complete silence* VINE *proceeds to fasten some of the gadgets on his special spacesuit, then methodically puts*

on and adjusts the atmospheric helmet mask. *He goes
to the side, right, and pressing a button switches on a
white spotlight focussed on the glass-cabin at the side
—the airlock. He enters it, drawing the doors to care-
fully behind him, presses another button inside, there is
a sizzling noise, and any loose draperies, etc. flutter as
the air from the airlock is pumped back into the ship.
Meanwhile* VINE *stands there brightly illuminated. So
soon as the pumping stops he is seen to open the outer
door after having tested the straps of his mask, the spot-
light on him as he goes, all watch him slowly descend-
ing the ladder into the outer darkness.*

    Silence.

    Curtain.]

    *   *   *   *   *

SCENE III
Desolation Corner.

[*Darkness; a desolate, arid waste of rocks and boulders
with here and there crater-like hollows in the midst
of rough, stony plateaux. Far behind is a faint outline
of harsh, low mountains: across and across the waste
blow wet, clinging mists in torn scarves and wisps and
streamers of vapour. The whole effect is in greys and
blacks, the only light available coming from an unshut-
tered window in the hull of the spaceship, one section of
which—twisted and torn, is visible in a corner (left)
of the stage.* VINE, *having preceded them to test the
atmosphere and ground surface, etc., is now standing
near the ship. Having signalled all's well to the others
who are waiting inside the* ARGONAUT *near the air-
lock, he runs up the ladder and opens the outer door,
gesturing them to come out. Then he presses a button
on the hull; at once a beam of a searchlight from the*

nose of the ARGONAUT *sweeps the stage, throwing sinister and hugely fantastic shadows until it comes to rest suitably on the ladder and its immediate neighbourhood.* SIR GIFFARD *is the first to descend, pompously and with extreme dignity, but brandishing a pistol, which spoils the gravity of the moment by going off suddenly, to* SIR GIFFARD's *obvious astonishment. As the pistol cracks and the sound echoes hollowly among the rocks, excited chatter breaks out, and one shrill cry, among the group which stands in the airlock cabin waiting to come out.* VINE *stands quietly by the foot of the ladder.* SIR GIFFARD *is now off.*]

SIR GIFFARD [*laughing sheepishly*]. If anyone else had done that, I should have called it careless, eh?

VINE [*curtly*]. Yes.

[*He continues to stand beside the foot of the ladder as the rest descend. First comes* LETTY, *coquettish in every movement to the admiration of the men; she clings to* SYLVESTER's *proffered arm. They touch the ground practically the same moment.* LETTY *shivers and draws a mackintosh about her, as if shrinking form the mists scudding by, and weighs heavily upon his protective arm.* SYLVESTER *stands silent, drinking in the details of all around, then, breaking the tension he declaims:*]

SYLVESTER. Are we the first who ever burst upon this silent ... ?

[*He stands enraptured, his imagination deeply stirred.* LETTY, *always flexible to a mood, adjusts her voice almost to a whisper as she clasps her arm afresh.*]

LETTY. Yes ... we *are* the first.

[BULLIVANT *comes briskly down the ladder bearing various impedimenta.* BONSOR *next descends and halts the company by his cry of—*]

BONSOR [*in worst pulpit manner*]. My friends [*looks round at every face, hollowed and contorted in the beam of the searchlight*]. Surely we must not let this moment pass without giving thanks to the Lord for our safety?

SYLVESTER. Beware of pagan worship! There may be native gods here. However, we certainly can thank Vine ....

BONSOR. In this strange and awful place, can we afford to be irreverent?

SYLVESTER. Can we ever? But there is no irreverence in truth: without our trusty Vine we should fall through the vasty deep of space ... ugh! A nasty mess!

[*LIMPETT is now seen descending the ladder very cautiously indeed. As soon as he is down, however, he begins giving orders to BULLIVANT in a rather bullying manner.*]

LIMPETT. Now, Bullivant, have you remembered Sir Giffard's air-cushion?

BULLIVANT. It's here.

LIMPETT. Good! Brought his tablets? Good! and his pills?

BULLIVANT. Yes, the whole bag of tricks.

LIMPETT. Right. Then bring the campstool here.

[*BULLIVANT does so, then busies himself otherwise.*]

SIR GIFFARD [*loudly*]. Limpett, come here!

LIMPETT. Yes, Sir Giffard.

SIR GIFFARD. We shall need the tent ... and the electric stoves .... Quick now! It's damn cold, standing about in this mist!

[*He stamps his feet. BULLIVANT hurries along and sets in the centre two big electric stoves designed specially to throw out heat widely in the open air. When these begin to glow, all the members of the party draw round them, setting their campstools in a close circle. General*] *conversation begins, during which* BULLIVANT *hands round weapons—one to each person—which are laid on the ground beside them.*]

VINE [*addressing all*]. Now there is no need for alarm. So far, we are all safe and sound. We shall have to take our bearings, and so forth, as so as we can. Luckily, conditions here seem not very different from on the Earth: there seems to be no difficulty about the atmosphere; the air is a trifle thin, but exhilarating; and we can move, see, breathe and hear quite comfortably. We have plenty to eat; and inside the ship at least we can keep warm. Quite soon now, sunlight may penetrate this darkness, and then for a time we can explore, until the sun's heat forces us back to the ship. Meanwhile, there may be dangerous creatures—we do not know; so these weapons are just a precaution. And we shall need to post a sentry to watch until it is light ... change every three hours. Of course, we do not know how long this night may be [*general apprehensive murmurs*], nor if dawn will ever come. Will you, Mr. Bonsor, take the first turn as sentry ... and you, Mr. Sylvester, the second?

SYLVESTER. Certainly.

BONSOR. I shall be very please to do so, Mr. Vine.

VINE. Good. Then, that's settled. Now, Mr. Bullivant is bringing round some hot soup. After that I think we might go back to the ship and finish the night's sleep.

[BULLIVANT *makes the round with the thermos flasks and cups. There is an air of revived hopefulness in the party.* VINE *disposes of his soup rapidly, rises and turns to* SIR GIFFARD.]

Sir Giffard, I must have a word with you.

[*They go aside to confer. Meanwhile* SYLVESTER *and*

BONSOR *are comparing their watches preparatory to*
BONSOR *beginning his sentry-go, when* SIR GIFFARD
is heard.]

SIR GIFFARD [*loudly*]. My God!

[SYLVESTER *and* BONSOR, *startled by the ejaculation,*
hurry round to where he is standing with VINE. BUL-
LIVANT *gets there too, but more quietly.*]

SYLVESTER [*abruptly*]. What's up?

[SIR GIFFARD *raises a deprecating hand. He looks*
very grave and almost mechanically takes a small
phial from his pocket, extracts a pill and swallows it.
Slight pause.]

Are you both dumb? What's the matter?

VINE. Yes, Sir Giffard. They must be told.

[*Slight pause.*]

LETTY [*clutching* SYLVESTER'S *arm*]. What is it?

[SYLVESTER *makes soothing gestures as to a child.*]

VINE. This is important. You all knew there were risks
in this journey.

[*A brief buzz of general comment;* VINE *raises his hand*
for silence, and proceeds.]

Our machine is [*pause*] severely damaged. [*Slowly:*]
We cannot return!

[*This announcement produces general consternation. All*
are badly shaken, but LIMPETT *shows it most.* LETTY
seems more buoyant than the rest, because her reporter's
instinct fastens upon what is evidently a whale of a
story, which causes her almost to overlook her own
personal danger.]

LETTY [*to* VINE]. Can I use the radio?

VINE [*curtly*]. No . . . that also . . . every kind of link we
had with the Earth is broken, at present. Later per-
haps, we may be able to re-establish contact.

SIR GIFFARD [*hiding any qualms of fear by an exaggerated magniloquence, coughs impressively, waits for silence, then says:*] Mr. Vine has told you one fact. I will remind you of another. We have reached the Moon ... a tremendous achievement! ... We are the supreme pioneers of mankind! ... and, remember, we are all British.

SYLVESTER. Hooray!

[*LETTY giggles.*]

SIR GIFFARD [*looks at SYLVESTER and LETTY for a moment with extreme distaste*]. British, I said ... and that means the stiff upper lip ... purpose, courage, determination ... gilt-edged success.

[*Pause. SIR GIFFARD smooths his moustache, complacently, looking round as for applause. SYLVESTER interjects:*]

SYLVESTER. Up the dividends!

BONSOR [*claps his hands, smiling*]. Yes, indeed! Excellent! They can't go too high!

SIR GIFFARD [*resuming*]. And how shall we maintain the success so far achieved? ... By doing our duty. Remember today we have added new territory to the Empire, new glories to the scroll of British enterprise, new ... new [*testily*]—

SYLVESTER. New pickings!

SIR GIFFARD. Yes, if you want the crude truth, new pickings. And why not? We have dared, we have sweated ... we claim our just reward.

BONSOR [*applauding, with enthusiasm*]. If I may add my humble tribute; we have been led here by the hand of Providence ... and, of course, the skill of Sir Giffard. Whatever may prove to be our lot in these dreary wastes—fire, earthquake, eclipse—

SYLVESTER. And things that go bump in the night . . . .

BONSOR [*resuming, skilfully*]. Yes, as you say, and wild beasts. And hunger, too—

VINE [*crisply*]. We have six months' rations.

BONSOR [*deflated*]. Oh!

[*He stops. The rest break out in exchanging congratulations upon the satisfactory food situation, which seems to cause them to forget other perilous uncertainties of their position.*]

SIR GIFFARD [*smugly*]. Of course, I have used foresight.

LETTY. Of course you have, Sir Giffard. You always do.

SIR GIFFARD [*receiving this public tribute with obvious satisfaction, beams at LETTY, then recollecting himself, says to LIMPETT in a business-like manner*]. Limpett, we must get on with my log. You have taken full note of all that has passed so far?

LIMPETT [*hesitant*]. Ye . . . ye . . . yes, Sir Giffard.

SIR GIFFARD. Good. Then come back with me to our quarters . . . . It's warmer there. I will dictate some instructions and notes for the ceremony. [*Again addressing the rest:*] At noon, Greenwich Mean Time, I shall hold a formal ceremony to annex this new territory to the Empire. I expect you all to attend.

[*SIR GIFFARD and LIMPETT go off, followed closely, but rather stealthily, by BULLIVANT. LETTY curls up close to the stoves, making notes, not without some sly occasional glances to the men-folk to see what they are doing. BONSOR, with fussy theatricality of pacing and gesture, makes a great show of taking up his position as the first sentry. Wearing his black clerical hat at a slightly rakish angle, he stands lugubriously immobile; his revolver, poised in amateur vigilance, glints in the light from the spaceship. Then he shivers, thinks for a*]

moment, quietly leaves his post and re-enters the ship.
SYLVESTER *goes across to* VINE.]

SYLVESTER. I don't know, Vine, how you manage to stand my brother-in-law's magniloquence. When it doesn't enrage me, it makes me flippant. I don't need to tell you, *his* Empire is bounce and baloney; the City is his guiding star. And so he contrives to dwarf this truly sublime adventure to the meanness of just ... a dividend-paying proposition.

VINE. That does not surprise me. We scientists do not often find an employer as big as the job he wants done. If Sir Giffard is, let us admit, sometimes ridiculous, there is all the more need for us to keep clearly before our eyes the ... [*almost shyly, after a hesitant second*] ... the vision splendid.

SYLVESTER. Yes. But I am afraid, Vine. Will those who follow us reject the craze for dividends, the lust for power, and every killing motive? If they do not, then this wonderful journey of ours will be in vain.

VINE. Honest research is never wasted. If we fail, others will succeed. Our job is to go ahead, taking no heed of the jungle-motive in high finance.

SYLVESTER. So you're an optimist too. "A man's reach should exceed his grasp, or what's a heaven for?" Eh?

VINE. Yes. We laboratory blokes can share in a poet's flight, as you are sharing ours.

[*During their conversation,* BONSOR *has returned; and* LETTY *has quietly crept up to them and is listening. Now she says:*]

LETTY [*archly*]. Exchanging confidences, Dr. Vine, in this dark, weird wilderness?

VINE. The one and only. Miss Mowbray. [*Pauses.*] Well, I must get back to my work.

[*He goes over to* BONSOR.]
Anything doing, Mr. Bonsor?

BONSOR. No. It is cold ... and lonely ... almost terrifying. But the Lord is my shepherd, you know.

VINE. Good!

[*He goes away and climbs into the ship.* BONSOR *now starts on a circular tour of the territory.*]

SYLVESTER. Are you feeling nervous, Miss Mowbray?

LETTY. Nervous! With you here. [*She looks up at him, archly*] ... and, of course, the Reverend Mr. Bonsor.

[BONSOR *having just passed them on his round.*]
He's not a bold, bad man ... or a poet.

SYLVESTER [*ambiguously*]. How do you know he is not?

LETTY. I am sure you *are*.

SYLVESTER. Which do you like best ... the poet ... or the bold, bad man?

LETTY. That's for you to find out. [*Giggles.*]

SYLVESTER [*quizzically*]. Would you like to hear some poems? [*Slight pause.*]

LETTY [*assents, purring, rubs her cheek softly against his, but finds it bristly*]. Oh! You've forgotten to shave!

SYLVESTER [*rubs his chin with satisfaction*]. Ah! You must learn to like your he-man rough ... and tough.

LETTY [*almost whispers, with more giggles*]. I do.

[*He picks up two or three cushions from a nearby heap, selects a suitably shadowed recess of the lookout rock, places the cushions, tests the corner for draughts, then triumphantly picks up one electric stove and transfers it to within warming distance of the nook he has made; i.e., near enough but not giving full illumination. Then he whistles softly and beckons to* LETTY, *calling quietly:*]

SYLVESTER. Letty ... Letty!

LETTY [*moving a little way towards him*]. Yes?

SYLVESTER [*child's play*]. He-man's cave!

LETTY [*scoffs*]. Huh! that's no cave ... and where's the he-man?

[*But she ventures nearer and he draws her in. They sit down comfortably, nestling together against the rock: now they are only vaguely outlined by the light from the stove. Sounds of whispered interchange, a giggle, and* SYLVESTER *is heard to say loudly:*]

SYLVESTER. You know you do!

[*Further slight sounds.* BONSOR *now approaches on his round, misses the stove from centre, peers round and at last catches sight of the alcove and the shadowy couple.*]

BONSOR [*quietly, to himself, with a chuckle*]. He's a quick worker! I couldn't have done better myself. [*Then loudly:*] Oh dear ... oh dear, dear, dear!

[*He drops his revolver with a clatter, then shines his torch on the delinquents, as he pretends to suppose them.*]

Really, Mr. Sylvester! I hardly know what to say.

SYLVESTER [*curtly*]. Then don't say it.

BONSOR. So unseemly ... at the best of times ... but now ....

SYLVESTER. Now what?

BONSOR. Here ... in this dark waste, so far from Earth ... facing the dread unknown ... to be ... well, cuddling ... you know what I mean.

LETTY [*kittenish, puts forward her head, so that her eyes gleam in the light from the torch*]. There's no harm in cuddling, Mr. Bonsor ... surely you know ... it's nice.

BONSOR. How should I, indeed, know anything of the kind?

LETTY. Well, Mr. Bonsor, after all ... even clergymen—

BONSOR [*moved to stronger protest, interrupts*]. As moral custodian of this expedition, I must insist—

137

SYLVESTER [*irritably*]. Go away, man!

BONSOR. If I go, it will be to acquaint Sir Giffard with the ... the ....

SYLVESTER. The what?

BONSOR [*hesitant*]. The ... the ... facts, you know.

SYLVESTER [*laughs, mocking him*]. That's all right, go ahead!

BONSOR. I will!

> [*With a show of determination, he turns, picks up his revolver and begins strutting towards the spaceship. At this moment he and LETTY and SYLVESTER see two strange figures standing silhouetted against the rapidly glowing light of the "lunar" dawn. These figures stalk gauntly towards them without a word, their faces expressing astonishment.*]

Good gracious! Moon-Men!

> [*So saying, BONSOR, brandishing his revolver, takes to his heels, rushes to the ladder and climbs quickly into the ARGONAUT. As he climbs, something drops from his coat at the foot of the ladder. From their corner, SYLVESTER and LETTY get up, come out and stare amazedly at the two strange figures.*]
>
> *Curtain.*]

*　　　*　　　*　　　*　　　*

SCENE IV

SIR GIFFARD MACKENZIE'*s room at the London office of* INTERPLANETARY DEVELOPMENT SERVICES, LIMITED.

> [*MACADAM, a fairly young, hard-faced but rather good-looking City Man, is sitting in the Managing Director's chair, reading correspondence. MACADAM touches a button and a voice replies.*]

VOICE. Is that Sir Giffard Mackenzie's office?

138

MACADAM. Yes. Who are you?

VOICE. B.O.F. News Agency here.

MACADAM. Well, I am Sales Macadam—Sir Giffard's deputy when he's away. What do you want?

VOICE. Is your office the headquarters of the INTER-PLANETARY DEVELOPMENT SERVICES?

MACADAM. We are the Head Office. Actually, I suppose the headquarters, just now, are somewhere in space—or on the Moon if the Managing Director has reached there yet. Of course, we can't know the actual speed the ARGONAUT is making.

VOICE. They have not reached the Moon.

MACADAM [*intently*]. Have you definite news?

VOICE. The ARGONAUT is down.

MACADAM. My God! Here, wait a moment. Don't go away. [*He calls to the outer office:*] Daphne, come in at once!

> [*DAPHNE, a pretty, young secretary-typist, comes in brightly with notebook and sits down in the chair beside the desk.*]

Daphne, the B.O.F. Agency has news of the expedition ... seems serious. Take down their message exactly as they give it. [*Presses button.*] Sorry to have kept you waiting, B.O.F. Now, tell me all you know ... dictation speed, please.

VOICE [speaking at dictation speed]. U.N.O. "Stratos" Radio-location at five o'clock this morning reported the whereabouts of the ARGONAUT, the spaceship of the INTERPLANETARY DEVELOPMENT SERVICES, LIMITED, which set out from London at twenty-one hundred hours last night with Sir Giffard Mackenzie, the famous financier, Dr. Wilbur Vine, the eminent scientist, and others on board. Stop. The ARGONAUT's objective was the Moon and this is the first voyage of the kind ever attempted by man. Stop. The course of the ARGONAUT was traceable until 4:36 this morning. Stop. After making a wide trajectory through the stratosphere into space, the ARGONAUT suddenly changed her course, taking a parabolic curve short of the Moon and back into the sphere of the Earth's gravitation. Stop. From the last bearings taken, it seems that the vessel has grounded on one of the small islands on the Outer Hebrides. Stop.

> [*Here* MACADAM *shows signs of great excitement, gets up and paces the room whilst he listens.* DAPHNE'*s note-taking, too, betrays nervous tensions.*]

Nothing more is yet known, for the landing—or, it may be, the crash, has evidently destroyed, or at least put out of action for the time being, all the ARGONAUT's radio communication instruments. Stop. In fact, no messages can be effectively sent to, or received from, the expedition at present. Stop. [*Slight pause; then the voice adds:*] That's all.

MACADAM. Thank you; that's plenty to go on with! Ring me again the moment you get any more, please. And I will let you know then what steps we are taking at this end.

VOICE. Right!

> [MACADAM *presses the button to close the telephone.* DAPHNE *is evidently glowing with excitement over her share in this big news.* MACADAM *stands for a moment or two thinking, then says, almost to himself:*]

MACADAM. Silly old windbag! This will teach him to strut around thinking himself God Almighty, only more up to date and twice as clever.

DAPHNE. Oo, Mr. Macadam!

MACADAM [*misunderstanding the ejaculation as a question without aspirate*]. Never you mind, Daphne. There's no time to waste. I shall want you to get the Air Ministry on the phone . . . I must talk to any high-up on duty there at the moment. Then get me Sir Iridene Kewte at Barts . . . then the News Editor of the *Evening News* and . . . and what's his name on the *Evening Standard* . . . and we mustn't forget the *Star*, of course. Oh, and after that, the B.B.C. and Movietone News. I'll take 'em all on this phone as fast as you can get them. We have to charter a hospital plane and organise a rescue party . . . and every minute counts! Now, step on it, Daphne; there's a good girl!

[*DAPHNE stiffens to her job, picks up the Telephone Directories, turns the leaves rapidly and lists the required numbers with swift efficiency, then begins at once to dial.*]

DAPHNE. Is that the Air Ministry? I want . . . [*her voice fades out . . . .*]

[*Curtain.*]

END OF ACT II

ACT III

SCENE I

Desolation Corner—the same morning.

[*The plateau at Desolation Corner at this time, which
seems like mid-morning, is less terrifying in aspect than
it appeared in darkness, but even in sunlight looks a
dreary enough waste of rocks and scree.* BULLIVANT
*comes down the ladder in his shirt-sleeves and dunga-
rees—the latter of dark blue and bearing* SIR GIFFARD's
own crest in silver on the left breast. BULLIVANT *pot-
ters around on various small duties, testing the elec-
tric stoves, and setting out cushions and campstools at
appropriate points. He is whistling softly as he works.*
BONSOR *is now visible, at first peering out of the air-
lock, then sidling down the ladder, looking around him
right and left as he comes towards the centre of the stage
rather apprehensively. He is still wearing his cleri-
cal collar and round, black hat, but now a thin black
alpaca coat instead of his clerical frock-coat.*]

BONSOR. This place looks better by daylight ... and the
air is quite balmy, you know. [*BULLIVANT says noth-
ing.*] So you're tidying up, Bullivant. Very good. Yes.
Were you ever a Boy Scout by chance?

BULLIVANT. No, Sir, I never had no times for games.
[*He picks up gingerly from the ground a rubber hot-
water bottle, which he holds out delicately on contemp-
tuous forefinger.*]
Is this yours, Sir?

BONSOR. Ah! My hot-water bottle. Very comforting
for sentry duty. I must have dropped it last night.

BULLIVANT. Yes, Sir, you were in a great hurry ... but
they seemed quite harmless.

BONSOR. Our planetary friends. Yes. I wonder what we

should call them. Not Lunatics ... no ... I suppose not ... Harmless? Perhaps: but you never can tell. I remember, the very mildest man in my congregation came for me with an axe, one Sunday morning just after my sermon—

BULLIVANT [*unsympathetically, interrupts*]. Aye, Sir, funny thing religion: it takes 'em all sorts of ways. But I don't need to tell you that, Sir. You know.

BONSOR [*doubtfully*]. Ye ... e ... s ... hrm. By the way, Bullivant, I have often thought that great men like Sir Giffard bear a tremendous burden. Don't you think so eh?

BULLIVANT [*edges away, BONSOR following, and is a trifle slow in replying*]. He treats me quite well, Sir.

BONSOR. Of course, of course ... a true gentleman ... a great gentleman ... so rich ... but not at all mean.

[*He looks narrowly at BULLIVANT, awaiting revelations. BULLIVANT looks at him rather sourly, but says nothing and straightens some cushions. BONSOR, determined to improve his opportunity, continues.*]

Last night, he was magnificent ... so courageous, yet modest ... the born commander, generous and gentle, but firm.

[*BULLIVANT still says nothing, but goes on with his work, though again begins to whistle softly a popular song in ironical comment .*]

And prudent, too, like all great leaders. [*Clutching the lapels of his coat, as if a stole, he beams benignly at the impassive BULLIVANT.*] I suppose, by the way, he *has* arranged for a rescue expedition to follow ours? [*Waits, but gets no reply.*] You don't know? [*Reassuringly.*] Yes, yes, I am sure he will have thought of everything.

BULLIVANT [*becoming almost loquacious*]. It's not for me to say, sir, but I expect you're right.

BONSOR [*cheered by this apparent confirmation, becomes even more friendly-confidential*]. Yes, you know, Mr. Bullivant, I have always found that a man of his kind, with vast interests, has the heart of a child.

BULLIVANT. Perhaps so, sir. He does seem a bit childish sometimes. [*He turns away with a suspicion of a smile.*]

BONSOR. Hardly what I meant. But certainly such men always rise superior to any circumstances, however adverse .... Ah, here comes Sir Giffard.

[*SIR GIFFARD now comes down the ladder. He is neatly dressed in rough tweeds, with tie, shirt and shoes all carefully harmonious and in beautiful condition; his iron-grey hair and slight moustache neatly brushed. The sunshine glistens on the platinum top of his very expensive walking-stick. He is smoking a slightly Holly-wood cigar. Being now in the rather glacial mood of the recently breakfasted wealthy Briton, he grunts at BULLIVANT and gives BONSOR a first curt nod, and then a grudging* "Good Morning." *Having heard* BONSOR's *flattering comment—as was intended—he struts accordingly.* LIMPETT *has followed close on* SIR GIFFARD's *heels, as usual. His Hitlerish moustache accentuates by contrast his somewhat bleary-eyed look and unhealthy pallor. He still wears his expedition costume—including revolver—but with the jacket thrown open at the neck; and he carries his inevitable notebook. Yawning as he comes on, he follows* SIR GIFFARD *wearily, dog-like.*]

SIR GIFFARD [*anxiously to* BULLIVANT]. Sylvester and Vine not returned yet?

BULLIVANT. No, sir.

SIR GIFFARD. They have been away nearly an hour. [*Testily:*] What's keeping them? [*Slight pause.*] You had better get that tent put up, Bullivant.

[*BULLIVANT proceeds to start the job.*]

BONSOR. Providence is looking after them, Sir Giffard.
We need not worry.

SIR GIFFARD [*grunts*]. Quick on the trigger has its advan-
tages ... but my brother-in-law ... no sportsman ...
and as for those scientist-fellows! ...

BONSOR [*ultra-delicately, as if grasping the nettle*]. Your
brother-in-law ... I fear [*he smiles uneasily*] ... hm ...
is too enterprising sometimes. You were not there
last night, Sir Giffard, to see ... hm ... but I did ...
the Moon-Men ... [*he giggles*] came only just in time.

SIR GIFFARD [*sharply*]. In time for what?

BONSOR. Better not, Sir Giffard ... far better not. Young
men ... and women ... and Nature. [*He punctuates
these comments with deploring shakes of the head.*] Alas!
The old, old story ... most regrettable.

SIR GIFFARD. Hm, another Sylvester incident. Psha!
I have no time for such nonsense. There is work to
do. I have to plan the administration of this new
territory.

BONSOR. Ah, Sir Giffard, then you *do* expect that we
shall be able to return to Earth after all?

SIR GIFFARD. That, sir, is quite irrelevant just now.
We are the first to land here, and of course I shall
formally annex the Lunar territory to the Empire.
Expansion ... always expand [*he draws himself up
and puffs out his chest*] ... that is my policy ... and it
pays ... handsomely!

BONSOR [*with an ingratiating cough*]. That reminds me,
Sir Giffard ... my little savings ... [*giggles*] widower's
mite ... could you spare me a small financial interest
in this undertaking?

SIR GIFFARD [*pauses to look at BONSOR calculatingly*]. Sir,
I deal in millions, not mites.

BONSOR [*anxious to persuade*]. My mite is not so very small, Sir Giffard. I have not buried my talent ... it has been out at high interest.

SIR GIFFARD [*almost heartily*]. That's another matter ... but I doubt if there will be any shares to be had. [*Calls:*] Limpett!

[*LIMPETT comes across quickly.*]

Will there be any INTERPLANETARY shares left available after we go to allotment?

LIMPETT. No, sir, not a fragment .... By noon on Wednesday everything will be snapped up ... and the shares will go to a very high premium.

SIR GIFFARD. Hm ... pity! I should have liked to oblige the Reverend Bonsor. We must encourage the Church ... one of the pillars of the State, eh? [*Easily:*] We must see what we can do for you, Mr. Bonsor. Make a note of that, Limpett.

BONSOR [*effusively*]. Thank you very much, Sir Giffard. I will give you my cheque now.

[*With animation, he pulls out his chequebook and fountain pen, plants himself against a rock and is about to write when thought strikes him.*]

But ... tchee! [*giggles*] ... there are no Banks here on the Moon!

SIR GIFFARD [*grandly*]. We shall soon change all that.

BONSOR. Why, of course you will. [*He writes the cheque and hands it over.*] There, Sir Giffard. My mite for the Empire. Make it mightier yet!

[*At that moment, footsteps are heard crunching the gravel. SYLVESTER and VINE come in, walking rapidly. SYLVESTER sees the chequebook flourished in BONSOR's hand and says to him:*]

SYLVESTER. Are you making an offer for this planet,

Reverend Sir? I bet my brother-in-law will not sell it, except at a fabulous profit. However, caveat emptor, as the Romans used to say .... City men eat parsons, you know.

BONSOR. You need not warn me, sir, that Greed is one of the capital sins. [*Significantly:*] As you well know, there are others. But I am seeking dividends [*slight pause*]. [*With the chequebook still in his right hand,* BONSOR *uplifts his left piously to the sky.*] ... to endow the great Mother Church, which will, I hope, glorify the Moon—

SIR GIFFARD [*interrupts*]. Yes, yes. [*Impatiently, to* VINE:] Did you find them ... those creatures?

VINE. Yes. We came upon them about half a mile away —but only the two we saw last night. They seemed to be reconnoitring this place, so we hid ourselves and have been watching them closely ever since.

SIR GIFFARD. What are they like? Could they be used for heavy manual labour?

VINE. Perhaps so. They looked rather gaunt, but wiry enough. Astonishingly like human beings. They seemed to be talking together, but of course we could not understand their language ... if it were that. And I fancy they were of different sexes, but that needs verification.

SIR GIFFARD. Sylvester might tell us: he is an expert. [*Turns to him.*] I have been hearing about last night's episode.

SYLVESTER [*innocently*]. I ask you, could I have left her alone with the Reverend Bonsor?

BONSOR [*with a show of indignation*]. Sir, no breath of scandal has ever—

SYLVESTER [*interrupts*]. Never?

BONSOR. If you mean those Dorcas meetings at the vicarage, that was idle village gossip. They were quite innocent ... it was all satisfactorily explained.

SIR GIFFARD [*loftily*]. Gentlemen, vicarage affairs need not concern us here. Our parish now is supra-terrestrial.

SYLVESTER [*pointing to BONSOR*]. So we are to treat him as one of the heavenly bodies. Well, let him behave accordingly.

BONSOR [*throwing up his arms in impotent rage*]. I will listen no longer to this ... this profligate! [*He stalks off to the spaceship.*]

SYLVESTER [*calls after him*]. And don't go annoying the lady! Watch your step.

SIR GIFFARD [*impatiently*]. We shall have to investigate very thoroughly, Vine. In my view, a cautious, and even friendly approach to these ... these planetarians ... is indicated. And if, as I feel sure, the soil of this planet teems with rich and rare mineral deposits, we shall need to recruit a large force of labour on the spot.

SYLVESTER. Grand! A simple people, we trust. No trade unions, *no* Government controls, low wages, unlimited profits ... this wilderness a paradise now!

SIR GIFFARD. How you artist ne'er-do-wells hate the City! ... because we City men are practical. But I shall not tolerate your interference here. This is my greatest opportunity ... virgin territory. I will tolerate no cramping of enterprise by idealist cranks. Discipline—yes, and plenty of it. No pampering in wages, in hours; no limitation of profits; no taxation. These safeguards secured, with opportunities for ever-expanding profits, we capitalists—as they call us—are always generous ... generous to a fault.

[*Launched full tide upon an oration, he beams round with satisfaction. Whilst he is taking breath, LIMPETT*

148

hands him BONSOR's cheque. SIR GIFFARD scrutinizes
and hands it back with the comment:]

Hm! Quite a substantial amount. You gave him the
prospectus?

LIMPETT [slyly]. No, Sir Giffard. I gave him the works.

SIR GIFFARD. Good! Now go in and make out his receipt.

[LIMPETT goes off to the ship. LETTY has been walking
hither and thither, full of curiosity, observing closely
and making rapid entries in her notebook. Now she
trips into the centre of the stage. She is dressed brightly,
and bubbling with joie de vivre; she adopts a playful
archness, especially aimed at captivating SIR GIFFARD.
She has evidently been fascinated by the sight of the
cheque, and looks eagerly after LIMPETT's retreating
figure.]

VINE. Good morning, Miss Mowbray.

SYLVESTER. Salutations, loveliness!

SIR GIFFARD. How do you do?

[LETTY responds with a charming smile. VINE now
leaves them and climbs up the neighbouring rock from
which he surveys the landscape with his binoculars.]

LETTY. What's he doing up there?

SYLVESTER. That's his observatory. We have to watch
out for the natives.

SIR GIFFARD [affably explains]. They may be dangerous.
I will join Vine and help him spy out the land.

[He goes to the rock, but after a feeble attempt to climb
it, gives up and stands puffing.]

LETTY. I don't believe those natives we saw last night
are dangerous. They looked perfect dears.

SYLVESTER. Dears be blowed! Playing gooseberries.
There were the Time, and the Place, and the Loved
One, all together ... and, by God, they must come
and spoil it!

149

LETTY. You have forgotten. The Reverend Bonsor took a hand.

SYLVESTER. Very well, so will I.

[*Taking* LETTY'*s hand, he strokes it, and then her head, gently; to which she responds, purring. Encouraged, he presses her head towards his own, whispering.* LETTY *begins to play with his tie, smoothing his lapels, and so on.*]

LETTY [*fondly*]. Silly Sylver!

SYLVESTER. Not at all. It was very clever of me to meet you here.

[*In the midst of this by-play,* LETTY *notices* SIR GIFFARD, *who is sitting alone by the rock apparently lost in thought. She begins to disengage her hand and head from* SYLVESTER'*s touch, and soon to talk loudly and enthusiastically in laudatory terms about* SIR GIFFARD.]

LETTY. So you pretend to have second sight; you saw me stowing away! No, my lad, don't deceive yourself. We have to thank Sir Giffard for this.

SYLVESTER. My wonderful brother-in-law.

LETTY. Yes, he *is* wonderful!

SYLVESTER. Now you're joking. You don't mean that.

LETTY. I do.

[*Out of the corner of her eye she can see* SIR GIFFARD *pretending to write in his notebook, but obviously listening with both ears.*]

Think Sylver, of what he is ... and what he has done.

[SYLVESTER *makes no reply, but recaptures and fondles her hand.*]

LETTY. I do believe you are jealous. Look what he has done for us!

SYLVESTER [*with some show of temper*]. Yes, landed us ... and stranded us ... good and proper!

LETTY. He provided the capital.

SYLVESTER. Other people's capital.

LETTY [*still with an eye upon* SIR GIFFARD]. Well, what-
ever you say, he is a great captain of enterprise. His
plans are colossal, and he can carry them. He is em-
peror of the air already, and on the way to be coming
tomorrow's architect of the Cosmos.

[SYLVESTER *sits back and lets out a sudden howl of
laughter, wipes his eyes, etc. When he has recovered
he says, playfully:*]

SYLVESTER. That's a modest claim, Letty. Why not call
him Conqueror of the Cosmos?

LETTY [*patiently, as to a naughty child*]. All right, you
may laugh. Perhaps you will not believe me, Sylver,
but, although he dislikes me, I admire him more
than I can say.

[*With a sidewise glance, she is watching* SIR GIFFARD
to see if he is reaching favourably.]

And if we do get back, I am going to write such a
biography of him as never was!

SYLVESTER. Very well, Letty. You do that, and I will
write the *true* chapter. The story of this great baronet,
arch-parasite of our time, grabbing his millions from
the pockets of his work-people and the scanty savings
of foolish clerks and widows; master of every mean
and petty device to extract tribute from all and give
little or nothing in return; the upright and steadfast
member who sits in Parliament to misrepresent the
people and load the dice of legislation always and
without exception to his own advantage. A great
gentleman, indeed! He—

LETTY [*interrupts*]. Stop, Sylver, stop!

[*She has seen* SIR GIFFARD *reacting to* SYLVESTER'S
*attack. He has risen to his feet, face empurpled with
rage, hands clenched, and only the necessity not to*

reveal himself has kept him from rushing to denounce his worthless young brother-in-law.]

A clever piece of invective, Sylver, but you know it isn't true. Mere Hyde Park bombast. Why, Sir Giffard has made millions. [*Slight pause, then impressively, in an awed whisper, she repeats:*] MILLIONS!

SYLVESTER [*savagely*]. Blast all women who worship money!

[*Brushing past her roughly, he strides over to the rock, climbs it rapidly and stands beside* VINE *on its summit. Meanwhile,* SIR GIFFARD's *features have been registering extreme satisfaction in listening to* LETTY's *testimonial. Now he stands for a moment looking at her, rubs his hands, then goes quietly back to the spaceship. On the way he meets* LIMPETT.]

SIR GIFFARD. Where's Bullivant?

LIMPETT. He's in the cabin, getting lunch ready, Sir Giffard.

SIR GIFFARD. Right. And don't forget. Have everything ready for the ceremony. My speech begins at noon.

LIMPETT. Very well, Sir Giffard.

[*The baronet ascends the ladder and disappears into the spaceship.* LIMPETT *picks up a campstool and plants it near* LETTY, *who is restoring her equanimity and complexion with powder and lipstick. She motions to him to sit closer beside her, which he does with alacrity, puffing the while at an outrageously large and vulgar calabash pipe. He is still wearing his expedition rig-out. After looking round a trifle apprehensively and seeing no one within range—the top of the rock cannot be seen from where they are sitting—he greets her with a familiar leer.*]

Well, my girl, how are things going?

LETTY [*still rather irritated by* SYLVESTER's *abrupt with-drawal*]. Oh, so-so. [*She taps with her foot, vexedly.*]

LIMPETT [familiarly, putting his arm round her waist]. Aren't you pleased to be here?

LETTY [*unwinding his arm*]. Don't, Joe, anyone might see you.

> [LIMPETT *looks sulky as she proceeds:*]

Well, you certainly managed to get me here all right; but where do we go from here?

LIMPETT. Don't you go blaming me, Letty. You pestered me to let you come.

LETTY. All right. But you were more than a bit clumsy, you know, stowing me in that locker with all those gas masks and junk.

LIMPETT. How the hell could I know you were going to tumble out like that?

LETTY [*recollecting, rubs the affected part*]. I should say tumble. [*Laughs.*] I've a bruise on my ——. Joe, do you remember that room at Anglesey? That was stuffier still.

> [*They both laugh. He bends over and kisses her fiercely. She puts up a warning finger. She is now in a very practical mood.*]

Just now, Joe, I began giving Sir Giffard the treatment. He sat round there behind the tent—thought I couldn't see him—and I gave him the great man stuff in headlines. His ears flapped; you could almost hear him purring. [*She assumes a look of stupid-innocence, then, simpering:*] I think, Joe ... I think he is beginning to like me a little, [*reverts to her hard-boiled manner*] the old so-and-so.

LIMPETT. That's fine. But what's the next move, Letty? We must settle it now. The old buzzard is always on the alert, and he mustn't suspect us of ... er ... any monkey-business.

LETTY. Would you be surprised if he tried something of the kind on me? I shouldn't. There's a glint of lechery in his eyes now and again which bodes a girl no good, if I know anything.

LIMPETT [*with a twisted smile*]. I'm counting on that ... and we shall expect him [*puffs at his pipe*] to be [*pause, with pipe raised in his hand*] very generous!

LETTY [*repeats*]. Very generous!

[*They look at one another, then laugh, derisively in unison. LIMPETT draws her to him rapidly, gives her a swift hug, then slaps her behind.*]

Don't, Joe, that hurts.

LIMPETT. You wait till we get back, my girl .... I'll show you!

LETTY. [*the wide-eyed, if mocking, innocent again*]. Oh! ... will you, Joe?

[*A gong sounds. At this moment SYLVESTER and VINE, who have descended from the rock, pass by on their way to the ship. They have come up quietly and it is clear from SYLVESTER's expression as he looks at LETTY that he has heard and seen enough to understand the relation of these two. For him, LETTY's spell is broken; his contempt is evident. He follows slowly in VINE's wake to the spaceship. LIMPETT gets up from his campstool, knocks out his pipe.*]

LIMPETT. Did you hear the gong? Lunch is ready. Coming, Letty?

LETTY. Yes, I'll just put my hair straight, and be along in a minute.

[*LIMPETT goes up the ladder. LETTY remains seated for a moment, pensive. Then she gets up, yawns and stretches herself with sensual abandon, sighs, then gives*

*her version of the Sphinx's inscrutable smile, looking
into the future as well as the past. She turns halfway
towards the spaceship in time to catch sight of the male
native just emerging from behind a rock. He carries
an implement over one shoulder, his feet are bare, his
belted shorts somewhat tattered. His shirt, wide open
at the chest, shows him to be a fine figure of a man. He
is tall, bronzed, athletic-looking, and as he stands poised
in the sunlight, seems a very Greek God in LETTY's eyes.
She gives a little gasp and an exclamation of happy ad-
miration. For a brief while they stand immobile, silent,
feasting eyes upon one another. Then she beckons to him
knowingly. He approaches her.*

    Curtain.]

    *   *   *   *   *

SCENE II

Desolation Corner—later the same morning.
[*The sun is high; Desolation Corner is bathed in light,
though wisps of mist still drift intermittently across
the scene. To the left, the battered hull of the space-
ship ARGONAUT, part buried in the sandy soil, gleams
metallic; to the right, a tent has been erected partly
shadowed by the lookout rock which towers above it.
For a few seconds the stage is empty ... then distant
voices are heard. BULLIVANT comes out of the tent with
a small roll of red carpet, which he unwinds to make
a path from the tent to the centre of the stage, where
is erected a small portable flagstaff, and, behind that,
a neat, one-tier platform with speaker's table attached.
Having completed the oratorical outfit by adding a
water carafe and glass, he goes into the tent again and
brings out a large portable gramophone in coloured plas-
tic, which he sets up against a corner of the rock; then*

he takes out and dusts some records. Whilst BULLIVANT
has been doing this, LIMPETT *has come down from the
spaceship carrying a documentary scroll, tied with red
tape and with heavy pendant seal attached; hanging
crooked over his arm is* SIR GIFFARD's *neatly furled
umbrella.* SYLVESTER, *walking with great strides fol-
lows and overtakes* LIMPETT *as he reaches the centre
of the stage.* SYLVESTER *stops abruptly, looks all round,
bends, and examines red carpet, scrutinises closely the
table and the flagstaff, then with great heartiness he
slaps* LIMPETT *on the back.*]

SYLVESTER. I say, Limpett ... this is great fun! [*Points
to scroll.*] What have you got there?

LIMPETT [*wincing from the backslapping, tries to be ultra-
dignified*]. This ... Mr. Sylvester ... is the Charter of
our Inter-Stellar Dominion.

SYLVESTER [*mock astonishment*]. No! But this is priceless.
Does Whitehall know?

[LIMPETT *makes no reply, but places the scroll conspicu-
ously on the table in centre.* SYLVESTER *goes over to*
BULLIVANT.]

Look here, Bullivant, I must be in on this. What have
you for me to do? [*Sees the gramophone and leaps to it.*]
Aye, this is in my line. [*Picks up record.*] Hm! Pomp
and Circumstance. [*Looks around.*] My God, I wish
we had a drum! [*Looks through some more records and
chooses one, saying:*] This beats Elgar hollow! [*Looks
round again, mock furtively, then seating himself on camp-
stool nearby, says melodramatically:*] I bide my time!

[*He remains there quiescent, a quizzical spectator,
wearing a look of patent innocence, his hands folded,
Buddha-like, on his stomach.* VINE *comes on, nods to*
SYLVESTER, *and at once climbs the lookout rock, where
he stands aloof and silent.* BONSOR, *seeming entirely*

in his element, hurries in, fussily. He is wearing his clerical hat, carries his hymn book in one hand, and has the Company receipt sticking out of his pocket. He approaches BULLIVANT *with genial condescension.*]

BONSOR. This is indeed the great day, Bullivant. We should be very proud and happy to be here ... to ... eh ... partake. [*Gleams benevolently upon him.*]

BULLIVANT [*impassive*]. Yes, sir.

[*He recedes to a point behind the table, looks butlerish.*]

BONSOR [*looks around*]. And where is Sir Giffard? [*Then in tones rich with welcome:*] Ah! Here he comes!

SYLVESTER [*remains seated*]. Hail, Caesar!

[*SIR GIFFARD emerges with great dignity from the tent, pacing slowly across the strip of red carpet to the flagstaff in the centre. He is dressed in the full regalia of the City—morning coat, striped trousers, even a carnation in buttonhole. He half turns to* BULLIVANT *with a magnificent gesture.* BULLIVANT *at once strikes three resounding blows upon the dinner-gong to indicate that the ceremony is about to begin; then, immediately, he picks up* SIR GIFFARD's *silk hat, polishes it deftly on his sleeve and hands it to* SIR GIFFARD, *who places it very carefully on the table.* SYLVESTER, *without rising, leans across the gramophone and at once there begins a very feeble and scratch recording of a British Colliery Brass Band playing "Rule, Britannia." This record runs for perhaps half a minute—whilst all the group except* SYLVESTER *stand sheepishly to attention—then the record trails off weezily into wailing silence.* SIR GIFFARD *blows his nose, coughs, takes a sip of water, looks round, then begins to speak—a little hesitatingly at first in these novel surroundings.*]

SIR GIFFARD. Ladies and—my friends. Here we are, safe and sound, on the first stage of our triumphant adventure. I will not weary you with the story of all the effort, the gigantic planning, the sleepless nights and laborious days which I devoted to this colossal enterprise. Scientific impossibilities have been hurled aside, the forces of nature grasped and bent to my will, and here we stand ... we stand ... [*hesitates*] on the ... on the—threshold ... of our ... yes ... magnificent task.

[*Obviously he is glad to have reached the end of that sentence. He mops his forehead slightly with handkerchief.* SYLVESTER *has risen from his seat and has come forward to watch and listen more closely: he now stands nearby, his mouth curved in a derisive smile.* BONSOR *applauds with loud handclapping.* SIR GIFFARD, *raising his hand for silence, proceeds:*]

It may have surprised you, my friends ... it did not, of course, surprise me ... that we have reached our objective, the Moon [*impressively*]. We have spanned those dizzy distances in, as it were, a flash. There are great strategic advantages in making the Moon our first base of operations. Can you not already see the great chain of our Company's trading stations linking every planet from the Moon to Pluto, our argosies flashing through space, faster than light, bearing precious freights for our new Stellar Empire.

[*He stops to take breath and a sip of water. Before he can go on,* SYLVESTER *has come forward, seemingly full of exultant appreciations. He cries out:*]

SYLVESTER. Hurrah! Good old Tennyson knew his onions! [*Then, with some overstress he declaims:*]

For I dipt into the future, far as human eye
    could see,

Saw the Vision of the world, and all the wonder
    that would be;
Saw the heavens filled with commerce, argosies
    of magic sails,
Pilots of the purple twilight dropping down
    with costly bales.*

BONSOR. You recited that very nicely, Mr. Sylvester,
    but I think you've interrupted Sir Giffard.
SYLVESTER. Sorry. Mack, your eloquence carried me
    away. . . .
SIR GIFFARD [*severely*]. Unfortunately, no . . . pray allow
    me to proceed.
BONSOR. Hear, hear! Sir Giffard! We are all ears.
SIR GIFFARD [*takes up the thread of his discourse*]. So, my
    friends, my bold vision of cosmic travel is beginning
    to be realised. We have taken the first step. Now I
    will tell you what must be done to turn this grand
    adventure into an eminently practical . . . and what
    is more . . . a thoroughly profitable enterprise. My
    plans are these. [*He consults his notes.*] First: We must
    have armaments . . . colossal armaments . . . and be
    ruthless to all enemies.
SYLVESTER [*as if chanting responses to a Litany*]. Death
    and Dividends.
SIR GIFFARD [*sweeps on, with comment*]. We will have no
    aliens on our planets.
SYLVESTER [*in mock contempt*]. Blasted foreigners!
SIR GIFFARD. We will have no democratic nonsense here.
SYLVESTER. Bravo. Hang all agitators.

* ["Locksley Hall," stanzas 60–61.]

SIR GIFFARD [*smirks in reply*]. Only the planets will be allowed their revolutions.

> [*BONSOR applauds this quip with guffaws. LIMPETT echoes applause sycophantically.*]

SYLVESTER. Utopia ... very limited!

SIR GIFFARD. We need no U.N.O. here!

SYLVESTER. No policemen?

SIR GIFFARD. Certainly not. Here we shall enjoy the full blessings of unrestricted private enterprise. What did Gladstone say in—

SYLVESTER [interrupts, speaking with deliberation]. A distinguished statesman very properly observed: If everybody would only agree to have nothing to do with anybody, then confidence would be completely restored.

> [*BONSOR chuckles.*]

SIR GIFFARD [*pompously*]. We have our mandate ... rest assured of that!

BONSOR. Don't you think, Sir Giffard, it would be rather a bright idea to have the Cosmos floodlit every night? [*Pats his share certificate and adds, with roguish smile:*] I am sure the shareholders would like it.

SIR GIFFARD [*accepting his absurdity*]. Hm! Ha! Limpett, make a note of that. [*Clears his throat ... to all:*] Later I will tell you more of my plans. now I will only add [*drawing himself up erect*] that I thank God—and [*bowing to BONSOR*] I say it with due reverence—I thank God that we do know how to play the game! [*Turning to BULLIVANT, he snaps out:*] Run up the flag! [*There is an awkward pause, then he repeats, more loudly:*] Run up the flag, I tell you!

BULLIVANT [*doggedly*]. No, sir.

SIR GIFFARD [*furious*]. Wh-a-a-t!

BULLIVANT. I can't do it, sir.

SIR GIFFARD [*amazed*]. You defy ME?

BULLIVANT. Yes, sir. [*Stands erect, setting his teeth, then bursts out with:*] Be damned if I will!

SIR GIFFARD. The man's insane!

BULLIVANT. No, sir. You said "no democratic nonsense." I won't stand for that!

SYLVESTER. Bravo! Bully for all!

BONSOR. Dear, dear! Bullivant gone bolshy. Tck! Tck! [*Shakes a grieved head.*]

> [*BULLIVANT says no more. He strides off and climbs up into the ship.*]

SIR GIFFARD [*deflated, turns to LIMPETT*]. You might run up the flag, Limpett.

LIMPETT [*leaps to it*]. Certainly, Sir Giffard.

> [*In silence he takes out from a case the silken House Flag of INTERPLANETARY DEVELOPMENT SERVICES, LIMITED—a blue ground on which the major planets swim in space with a small Union Jack in one corner. The flag is raised and flutters at its peak. Meanwhile LETTY has come in and is seen taking Leica pictures of the ceremony. She is closely followed by IOLAIR, who gives her a playful slap, causing her to make a half-turn towards him, whist she says with a giggle:*]

LETTY. Don't do that! I'm busy.

IOLAIR [*in Gaelic (translate)*]. My lovely one!

> [*EALA rushes in and madly attacks LETTY, clawing her and tearing her scarf from her throat.*]

EALA [*in Gaelic (translate)*]. You evil woman! He is my man!

> [*She makes another effort to claw LETTY, who gives a little shriek, but IOLAIR pulls her away. During the scuffle, VINE has climed into the midst of the rock. He*]

161

stalks authoritatively into the midst of the group, observing EALA and IOLAIR very closely.]

VINE [*turns to SYLVESTER*]. What do you make of them, Sylvester?

SYLVESTER. They look almost human to me. But [*mischievously*] why not ask Miss Mowbray. She's a reporter.

VINE [*almost to himself*]. I believe they are human.

SYLVESTER. Impossible!

[*But he paces thoughtfully to and fro, looking keenly at the islanders. SIR GIFFARD is being tended in a corner by LIMPETT, who hands him his pills and a glass of water. EALA, still held back by her man, glowers hatred at LETTY, who sits down on a campstool and with a show of composure powders her nose. She makes a moue at EALA, but gives IOLAIR a languishing smile. At this EALA breaks loose and runs off stage crying: IOLAIR follows, calling after her:*]

IOLAIR. Eala! Eala! [*In Gaelic (translate):*] Come back!

VINE [*watches the islanders vanishing into the distance then gives a start of surprise*]. Ah! that's it ... Gaelic!

[*SYLVESTER, who has strolled after the islanders, also watches them disappear, then returns.*]

Sylvester, there's something very odd here. I don't believe we've landed on the Moon at all!

[*Leaving SYLVESTER staring at him, VINE hurries off and goes up into the ship. BONSOR now comes up to LETTY, beams benignly upon her and pats her solicitously on the shoulder.*]

BONSOR. You must be more careful, Miss Mowbray. I can see I shall have to take you in hand.

LETTY. Oh, Mr. Bonsor, I wish you would!

[*BONSOR whinnies appreciatively and pats her hand. SIR GIFFARD has now pulled himself together, has*

*resumed his silk hat and gloves and now stands
fidgeting.*]

SIR GIFFARD. Have you taken down everything I said,
Limpett?

LIMPETT. Yes, Sir Giffard ... verbatim.

SIR GIFFARD. Let me have the script as soon as you
have typed it. But I won't have any of that imperti-
nent bounder's irrelevancies on record. [*Pompously:*]
It will be a historic document!

LETTY [*coming forward with most engaging smile*]. Sir Gif-
fard, that report will be priceless—

SYLVESTER [*laughs*]. Yes, indeed!

LETTY [*disregarding SYLVESTER's comment, continues*]. So
may I have a copy ... *please*, Sir Giffard ... for the
Gazette?

SIR GIFFARD. Well, my dear, if you can transmit the
copy to the *Gazette* at once [*laughs sarcastically*], I'll
give your rag the world rights. But I fancy the *Gazette*
has no agency on the Moon. Now, if we get back, in
three months' time your paper, like all the rest, will
have to take its cosmic news from my sole agency,
here or on Venus or Mars. It's all worked out.

LETTY [*wide-eyed*]. How wonderful! You *are* a Colossus!
     [*SIR GIFFARD receives this comment with calm satis-
     faction.*]
I must take a picture of you like that ... but do stand
beside the flag.

SIR GIFFARD. Very well.
     [*He ranges himself accordingly, and LETTY judges her
     camera distance. It happens that the whole party is
     grouped sufficiently near SIR GIFFARD. LETTY snaps
     her picture.*]

LETTY. Good! Do you know what I've done—I've got
you *all* in my picture!

SIR GIFFARD [*annoyed*]. You must not use that snapshot for the Press. I forbid it.

SYLVESTER. No. And I'll see that you don't. We have our feelings, too.

BONSOR. Oh, what a pity. Such a nice family party!

[*There is an uncomfortable pause; then the momentary hush is broken by the entry of a tall, lean, bronzed Don Quixote-like figure, with long white-yellow hair, a straggling pointed beard; he is wearing linen shorts, open-necked blue shirt, a white coat and sandals, and carries a rather drooping panama hat—he looks, in fact, somewhat like an R.B. Cunninghame Graham rather gone to seed. He comes forward in dignified manner, smiling and courteous, and steps towards SIR GIFFARD. He speaks a scholarly pure and perfect English without accent.*]

BERTRAM. Am I right, sir, in thinking you are the leader of this . . . expedition? I am Bernard Harrington-Bertram, at your service.

SIR GIFFARD [*impressively*]. Yes—I am Sir Giffard Mackenzie.

BERTRAM. Of INTERPLANETARY DEVELOPMENT SERVICES? Good! I have come to give you some information.

SIR GIFFARD [*his surprise and excitement mounting*]. Information? But how have you got here? You can't be one of Johnson's group. They bragged about beating me to it, but they haven't the guts . . . or the ship. [*With rising asperity:*] What are you doing here?

BERTRAM [*suavely*]. I am an ornithologist. It is my life's work. These islands are full of rare birds.

[*Stupefaction is visible on the faces of all the members of the expedition present . . . they gasp in broken phrases.*]

SIR GIFFARD. Islands!

BONSOR. Impossible!

LIMPETT. Absurd!

SYLVESTER. Fantastic! So Vine guessed right.

SIR GIFFARD. What do you mean, sir? Islands ... do you know where we are?

BERTRAM. I ought to know. I have lived here for twenty-five years.

SIR GIFFARD [*scornfully*]. Twenty-five years ... nonsense! You are an imposter, sir! Let me tell you that mine is the first party to have landed on the Moon, and I reject absolutely your pretended priority.

BERTRAM. What did you say? On the Moon ... oh yes, the Moon, of course!

[*The absurdity of the situation gets the better of his courtesy, and he burst into hearty laughter. When he has recovered, and wiped his eyes, he says:*]

Please forgive me.

SIR GIFFARD. Explain yourself, sir. I see no cause for laughter in anything I have said.

BERTRAM. I do apologise. A natural mistake on your part. Indeed, the object of my intrusion here was solely to explain ....

SIR GIFFARD [*stiffly*]. Well, sir—

BERTRAM. Five minutes ago I was listening to a wireless message from London, reporting that the INTER-PLANETARY SERVICES atom-driven spaceship ARGO-NAUT, which set out on a journey to the Moon at nine o'clock last night, had been radiolocated throughout its course. By some inexplicable error the vessel had short-circuited somewhere beyond the stratosphere and had crash-landed on Muckle Flugga, one of the remotest islands of the outer Hebrides—where we are now, Sir Giffard. It was not known whether any members of the expedition had survived; but happily

I find you here, and all your party, I hope, safe and sound.

SIR GIFFARD [has been growing redder and more excited during this recital; by this time he is almost clutching as his throat and battling for breath]. Hebrides ... tcha! It's impossible. It can't be. The thing's been too well organised. My shareholders ... ten million pounds in this!

[BERTRAM *has spoken a few words aside, in Gaelic, to* EALA *and* IOLAIR: *the flood of* SIR GIFFARD's *excited comment continues:*]

You, sir ... this is a conspiracy! I warn you, Mr. Harrington-Bertram and your two curious-looking friends there ... to be very careful! Hebrides, indeed!

BERTRAM [*quite unmoved*]. Very well, listen for yourself ... perhaps you can still hear part of the news summary.

[*Turning aside the sleeve of his white coat, he uncovers a wrist-radio, adjusts it, and holds out his arm so that all may hear.*]

ANNOUNCER. ... and the rationing of manufactured goods for export may be introduced at any time. [*Pause.*] The controversy concerning the jurisdiction of U.N.O. over all interplanetary expeditions has been brought to a head by yesterday's dramatic news of the flight of spaceship ARGONAUT under the command of Sir Giffard Mackenzie. It transpires that no application had been made to the World Aviation Control Board for a licence to fly the ship, and as a result of strong criticism today in certain sections of the Press and in the House of Commons it seems likely that his first rash adventure of interplanetary travel may provide the stimulus for immediate legislation by the Security Council. The Stock Exchange Committee is meeting tomorrow to consider the advisability of annulling the proposed ten-million-pounds share issue (which, it was expected, would be several times over-subscribed) on the ground that the venture was undertaken without authority. If proceedings on this count are to be taken against the leader of the expedition the affair is likely to prove a cause célèbre of world importance. Unfortunately it is not yet know if any members of the expedition are still alive, but we have just been informed that a rescue plane has started from London Airport and should land near the wrecked ARGONAUT within the next few minutes to bring back any survivors. It is believed, by the way, that there was a woman stowaway on board. As already stated, the members of the expedition were: Sir Giffard Mackenzie, the multimillionaire financier; his brother-in-law, Mr. William Sylvester, the well-known satirical poet; Dr. Wilbur Vine, the eminent Anglo-American physicist and inventor; Mr. Anthony Jeffries, his scientific assistant; Mr. Joseph Limpett, Sir Giffard's private secretary; Mr. Bullivant, Sir Giffard's valet; and Mr. Eugene Bonsor, star reporter of the Daily Sphinx. [*Pause.*] In the lawn tennis finals at Wimbledon today . . . [*fades out*].

[*BERTRAM has switched off his wireless and begins to move off quietly, followed by EALA and IOLAIR. For a moment no one speaks. The announcer's reference to BONSOR has astonished everyone except, of course, BERTRAM, the islanders and BONSOR himself.*]

SIR GIFFARD [*to BONSOR*]. Is that true?

BONSOR [*smiling*]. Well, Sir Giffard, I am working under orders, but not holy.

SYLVESTER [*chuckles, comes forward and shakes hands with BONSOR*]. You know, Bonsor, your missionary zeal

167

was a trifle exuberant, but I couldn't help liking you. I felt sure you were too good to be true.

BONSOR [*beaming*]. I did my best, brother. I am glad you enjoyed my performance.

LETTY [*effusively*]. A very good act, cher colleague—you and your wasps and birds and repressions.

BONSOR. Did you ever read, Sir Giffard, Humbert Wolfe's quip about us? "You cannot hope to bribe, or twist, thank God, the British journalist." And you can't!

SIR GIFFARD [*hotly*]. So you're not a parson, but just another damned pressman! I consider, sir, you have behaved abominably . . . . You're a cad, sir . . . a bounder!

[*He turns on his heel and goes into the tent, LIMPETT following. SYLVESTER stands happily, hands in pockets, still grinning.*]

SYLVESTER [*to BONSOR*]. A nasty jolt for our new Stellar Dominion, eh!

BONSOR [abstractedly]. Oh . . . yes. Excuse me.

[*He has just noticed LETTY stealing after BERTRAM and guesses what she is after. He breaks away and races towards them. Both reach BERTRAM at the same moment. Each tugs at his coat to attract his attention, and both cry,* "Mr. Bertram." *He looks at them, rather bewildered.*]

BERTRAM. What do you want?

LETTY. Your wireless . . . .

BONSOR. Is it a transmitter, too?

BERTRAM. No.

LETTY. Damn!

BONSOR. Blast!

[*They are both very disappointed and annoyed. BONSOR turns to BERTRAM:*]

Where's the Post Office?

BERTRAM. There is none on this island. The nearest is on the mainland, many miles away.

BONSOR. Well, isn't there a motorboat?... or a jet plane? God! Surely there's some way of getting there quickly. This is the biggest scoop ever! I must get it across at once!

LETTY. I'm in this, too, Mr. Eugene Bonsor ... don't forget that!

BERTRAM. I'm afraid there is no way quick enough for you. That is why I live here ... it is so primitive.

LETTY. Are you quite sure?

BERTRAM [*courteously, smiling*]. Quite sure.

[*He raises his hat, and goes off, serenely calm, beckoning to* EALA *and* IOLAIR, *who follow in single file.*]

LETTY. Let's try Vine; he may be able to suggest something. I think he's in the cabin.

BONSOR. Right!

[*They hurry towards the* ARGONAUT, *but meet* VINE *coming down the ladder. Meanwhile,* SYLVESTER *pokes his head into the tent.*]

SYLVESTER. Look here, Mack. If a plane's coming for us, what about our luggage?

SIR GIFFARD [*comes out of tent,* LIMPETT *following testily*]. Yes, of course, I'm having that done. See to it, Limpett. Help Bullivant to get as much of our kit as we can take ready at once.

LIMPETT. Very well, Sir Giffard.

SIR GIFFARD [*stands brooding over his wrongs; looking at* SYLVESTER, *who is jauntily humming a tune, he snarls*]. What are you so pleased about? You don't seem to realise what's happening!

SYLVESTER. There's no cause for grumbling. We are all safe and sound, it's a lovely day, and we shall be back in London soon.

SIR GIFFARD [*gritting his teeth*]. Back in London. yes, and what then? Even if the prosecution they're hinting at comes to nothing, how am I going to face the City? If the Press gets wind of the Moon business, I shall be the laughing stock of the world! And the whole expedition's gone phut. I'm not even certain I can collect the insurance money for the ARGONAUT. But I planned everything perfectly ... nothing could go wrong ... nothing should have gone wrong ... nothing ... but our wonderful scientist ... the eminent Dr. Wilbur Vine ... just let us down.

SYLVESTER. There's nothing wrong with Vine .... He has done jolly well, considering the circumstances, and you know it.

SIR GIFFARD. I know nothing of the kind.

[*LIMPETT comes along carrying two bags. He sets them down and turns to SIR GIFFARD.*]

LIMPETT. Bullivant's disappeared, sir.

SIR GIFFARD. What do you mean, disappeared? [*Slight pause.*] Ah, sulking, I expect. Well, you must deal with the baggage yourself.

[*LIMPETT goes off for more. VINE meanwhile has come down from the ship. He looks steadily at SIR GIFFARD, then says quietly:*]

VINE. Let you down ... have I? [*Raising his voice.*] I want you all, please, to hear what I have to say.

[*He stands before them all in semicircle facing audience. LIMPETT stops shifting the luggage, and stands on the edge of the group.*]

Now, Sir Giffard, you say I have failed you. How? [*Looks firmly at SIR GIFFARD, who has no reply ready. VINE proceeds slowly:*] Whatever deflected us from our course was no negligence of mine. it must have happened whilst I was knocked out, unconscious. Sir Giffard, you owe me an apology.

SIR GIFFARD [*astonished*]. Apology—preposterous!

SYLVESTER. Of course you do, Mack. And I'll tell you something more. I hadn't had much of an opinion of you when we started ... never have had ... but this trip has been a revelation. Within these last few hours you have grown to full size. Perhaps it is inevitable that a financier, always surrounded by crooks and toadies and simpletons, should naturally become a bully, a braggart and a swindler. You and your Limpett there are fine specimens ... flowers of our civilisation!—

SIR GIFFARD [*interjects hotly*]. By God, sir, I'll make you pay for this!

[*LIMPETT says nothing, but his sickly smile shows a toothy hatred.*]

SYLVESTER [*sweeps on*]. You have a kind of courage or you wouldn't be here! But that's largely due to your cushioned experience and a lack of real imagination. Your boasted initiative and resource have their roots in egotism and greed ... your desire [*mockingly*] to benefit the human race is just a pretence of nobility which low cunning puts on when snouting for bigger dividends. You *know* you are great—the delusions of grandeur always get your type, and you begin fancying you're a Napoleon or Mussolini. Ha! Ha! But that joke is wearing out at last. Man is shaking free from the feudal tyrannies ... we always destroy dictators in the end. Oh, yes, you're clever in your nasty little way ... everywhere on Earth your well-proved recipes for grabbing wealth and keeping power are being clipped and controlled and outlawed ... so now you turn to the planets and the Cosmos at large to find new fields for exploration. Well, you've failed, and you'll go on failing, and I'm damned glad of it!

BONSOR. Hurrah! Fine! That's the stuff, Sylvester! I've got it all down, every word of it!

SIR GIFFARD. If you are to print that, or anything like it, I warn you ... the *Daily Sphinx* will hear from my lawyers ... and I'll break you, too .... Seditious lies! ... Criminal libel! [*Turns to* LETTY, *and achieving suavity again with an effort, says:*] I am sure Miss Mowbray can give a very different version. I might let you have that exclusive interview, my dear, after all.

LETTY [*enthusing*]. Oh, Sir Giffard, that will be splendid. Can I take it now?

SIR GIFFARD [*confidentially*]. Better wait a little. Come and see me early tomorrow ... you shall have all you want.

LETTY. You are very kind, Sir Giffard. It's a bargain. I will.

[*They shake hands on it, he very courtly.*]

BONSOR. Well, you can count on the *Sphinx* publishing all the facts, Sir Giffard—threats included. And we shall probably publish a chart—of the Moon.

[*There is suddenly the sound of an airplane coming to the island circling round and then landing. All the group except* BULLIVANT *stand listening beside the heaped-up baggage, waiting, expectant. After a few seconds unfamiliar voices are heard, then* BERTRAM'*s.*]

BERTRAM. This way! I will take you to them.

[*He comes into view in company with an air* PILOT *and a* NURSE.]

Here they are.

SIR GIFFARD [*comes forward to do the honours*]. Ah, yes
    ... so the plane's here. But we've no injured for you,
    Nurse. All here are sound and well.

NURSE [*smiles*]. That is good. I am glad, sir.

PILOT [*bluff and hearty, goes up to SIR GIFFARD and shakes
    him by the hand very fervently*]. Sorry you crashed, Sir
    Giffard. Wonderful effort, though. The whole world
    is aflame to see you!

SIR GIFFARD [*erect again, twirls his moustache ends*]. Ah,
    yes, of course.

PILOT. Well, sir, if you're ready, we are.

SIR GIFFARD. There is only the baggage to check. [*Casts
    his eye over the heap.*] Limpett, where's my red brief-
    case ... you know, it's most important.

    [*All stand waiting, then begin turning over the bags
    in search.*]

LIMPETT. It's not here, Sir Giffard. I remember now,
    I couldn't find it when I was looking for bullivant,
    and your cabin was locked.

SIR GIFFARD. It's most important ... all my documents
    ... *I must have it!*

    [*BULLIVANT now appears coming down the ladder; but
    this a different BULLIVANT, straight from Savile Row,
    the perfect Foreign Office official.*[

    Good God! Who's that? It *can't* be Bullivant!

SYLVESTER. It is; and very nice, too.

BULLIVANT [*coming towards them, displays the red morocco
    briefcase which he is carrying. Speaking authoritatively,
    he asks:*] Is this yours, Sir Giffard?

SIR GIFFARD. Yes, of course. Give it to me at once.

BULLIVANT [*makes no move to do so*]. You admit this is
    yours, Sir Giffard?

SIR GIFFARD. You know it's mine.

173

BULLIVANT [*approaches close to* SIR GIFFARD *in a very deliberate manner*]. Yes, Sir Giffard. It is yours. I have examined its contents. Are all the documents yours?

SIR GIFFARD [*hesitant*]. I . . . well . . . .

BULLIVANT [*proceeds*]. They are. And they constitute a record of the most damnable conspiracy . . . plans for the entire and final enslavement of the human race by a very small group of unscrupulous financiers, super-Fascists, of whom you are a leading member. Your scheme for interplanetary dominion —as these documents show—was to be the pivot of your plan. Your group have plotted to destroy the United Nations Organisation. As accredited representative of the International Police Force, I hereby arrest you, Sir Giffard Mackenzie, in the name of the United Nations; and I call upon you to submit yourself to trial for your crime. [*Takes warrant out of his pocket.*] This is my warrant. [*Then he turns to the* PILOT *and says:*] Take this man into custody . . . and his secretary here, Mr. Joseph Limpett. The three others were arrested in London, New York and Buenos Aires this morning.

[*During the accusation and arrest* SIR GIFFARD *has been showing signs of extreme agitation. Now he begins to clutch at his throat.*]

SIR GIFFARD [*wildly*]. My heart . . . oh, brandy, please . . . my heart!

BULLIVANT [*unmoved*]. Take him away!

[*Whilst* SIR GIFFARD *is being carried off groaning and staggering, an abject caricature of his former self,* LIMPETT *dashes off behind the rocks. No attempt is made to capture him.* BULLIVANT *to* PILOT:]

We need not worry about him now. He cannot escape. We'll get him.

[*He, the* PILOT, *the* NURSE, *and* SIR GIFFARD *go out of view. There are left for a moment in the centre of stage,* VINE, BONSOR, SYLVESTER, *and* LETTY.]

VINE [*picks up his bag*]. How could I have known? Have we scientists a duty besides our research? [*Goes off, thinking deeply.*]

LETTY [*to* BONSOR]. Heavens, what a scoop!

BONSOR [*generously*]. Let's share it.

LETTY [*throws her arms round* BONSOR's *neck, and kisses him*]. We will.

[*They pick up their bags and go off gaily.*]

SYLVESTER [*looks at the flag, hanging limply on its staff— smiles sourly*]. So that WAS the Cosmic Empire! [*He follows the trail of the rest.*]

[*For a second or two the stage is empty and silent, dominated by the broken hulk of the* ARGONAUT, *overshadowing one corner. Then the figures of* EALA *and* IOLAIR *are seen coming out of hiding from behind the rocks.* IOLAIR *stops to the right of centre ...* EALA *glides lightly to centre, looks around, then snatches the flag from its staff and ties it round her neck in imitation of* LETTY's *scarf, and draws* IOLAIR's *attention to it. Then she runs back to him, and they go off, with his arm protectively round her.*

Curtain.]

THE END

175

Short Stories

ERNEST

"Good Morning!"

It was a queer gurgling kind of greeting. I looked up from my desk, but I was alone.

"Good Morning!"

Again the greeting, now somewhat peevish and still gurgly. Then, again looking up, I saw, to my astonishment, just above my head, some six inches away, supported upon the merest wafer of a shelf, a large glass bowl hazily gleaming through what I would call the misty atmosphere of the Astral Plane. This bowl reminded me of the Cheshire Cat in *Alice's Adventures in Wonderland* who would appear from nowhere, then disappear as unexpectedly. I was not surprised at this moment of Clairvoyance but what did surprise me was the glass bowl with water in it and a large, wistful-eyed, open-mouthed Goldfish who had apparently greeted me.

This Fish was looking at me in a forlorn manner and I felt it would have been discourteous of me if I had rubbed my eyes as though I did not believe in what I saw, I therefore greeted him as he did me.

"'Er, good morning; I really did not see you at first."

The Fish seemed to sigh; for some ripples stirred the water and it opened its mouth, paused and then:

"I have been here for years and years but you have never noticed me; I have always said 'good morning' when you came in."

I did not know how to reply, one is not clairvoyant all the time and really who would expect to see an astral bowl with a Goldfish just above one's head.

[*Catalogue and Review* (London: Atlantis Bookshop, 1947), pp. 3–4.]

The Goldfish continued: "My name is Ernest and I have been trying to get out ever since I have been here, swimming round and round and round; nobody to talk to, nobody who would care what I was thinking, feeling; and I want to know so many things!"

This was uttered in such a plaintive tone that I felt most sympathetic and the unusual situation of listening to an astral Goldfish was becoming familiar.

"I am sorry for you, but how did you get there?"

"That is a mystery to me, too, all I know is some memory that is so long ago that I can't remember"— it looked at me vaguely—"I'm sure I was somewhere before I was here, that is all." Ernest looked inquiringly as though he expected me to solve his problem; I had no reply to give.

He waited—then the large innocent eyes gleamed: "I believe I came here because I wanted to know!"

"Know what?" I asked.

"Why everything there is to know!"

"That is a great deal for a small Goldfish," I smiled.

"Small? Am I small? What do you mean by small?" Ernest almost gasped. Then I realised how lonely Ernest was; he had no way of comparing himself with other goldfish but he certainly did have great ambition.

"Well," I said, "*small* is a relative term, it means 'to compare oneself in size to something else'; you said you wanted to know everything; everything's a lot, you must choose something out of everything, something that will help you; for instance, you want to get out of that bowl, how do you think you can do that? If you leave the bowl you will be out of your natural element and will die, and I don't think you want to die."

The doleful expression returned to his eyes. "I feel

all tangled up. I can't get out and I really don't know what to choose and I certainly don't wish to die."

Now what could I say to bring in metaphysics and biology and discrimination to a mysterious Goldfish swimming forlornly round and round his crystal prison?

I thought for a moment, then believed I had the solution.

"Listen! as you have probably noticed, I am preparing an Occult Catalogue and suggest that as the lists are prepared, you read the titles and as I describe the works you will receive some idea about the nature and meaning of things."

Ernest's response was interesting and slightly absurd, he waved his delicate fins and golden tail, rippling the water so that some danced out of the bowl but vanished before I was sprinkled.

"Oh thank you, thank you very much," he bubbled; then, "I will—" at that moment the vision of excited Ernest vanished, and so far as I was aware, had a slightly fantastic episode.

ERNEST AGAIN

I had forgotten the existence of Ernest when he made his reappearance; or perhaps it would be better to say, I again became clairvoyant and aware that just a few feet above my head on the almost imperceptible shelf was a gleaming astral glass bowl with a golden fish swimming in it.

I had completed about half of my Catalogue and it was early afternoon when I heard the liquidly gurgling voice of Ernest greet me—"Good afternoon."

I looked up and recalled that grotesque incident of some weeks ago; I greeted him and was astonished to notice that a change had occurred; for Ernest was no longer the innocent and appealing little character who wanted to know. Ernest had definitely changed; this was a somewhat sophisticated, slightly aggressive intellectualised little fish.

Ernest had acquired, somehow or other, a pair of horn-rimmed spectacles; his golden scales had an untidy look; his fins had lost their neat, clean-cut lines; but his eyes, slightly magnified through the ridiculous lens of his spectacles, had a most keen expression.

"How you have changed," I exclaimed, but I did not add for the worse; his innocence had possessed a certain charm but this more mature Ernest had lost this appeal.

Ernest smiled. It is difficult to describe a smile on a fish but the impression Ernest conveyed was a smug smile, an irritating, patronising smile. "And I feel different," he said.

If Ernest could have stretched out a fin and patted

[*Catalogue and Review* (London: Atlantis Bookshop, 1947), pp. 16–17.]

me on the shoulder I am sure he would have done so. "It's reading all those books; I have been watching you and have memorised all the titles. I know about Anthropology, Archaeology, Alchemy ... Numerology." Ernest repeated alphabetically as far as I had reached in the Catalogue. He seemed to strut slightly as he swam, a difficult feat, but he certainly conveyed this attitude.

"I understand nearly everything now: the meaning of this and that; life, love, good and bad, large and little"—I interrupted—I had forgotten I was talking to a goldfish; I had forgotten how extraordinary the situation was; Ernest was no mirage of the mind and I was getting annoyed.

"All the problems that have tried and tangled the philosophers for ages you have untied?" Then I suddenly realised the absurdity of all this; to get angry with probably a figment of my imagination was nonsense; nevertheless there was Ernest in a glass bowl happily swimming and self-satisfied that the mere mass of information had solved his problems, I realised that all of us were in a similar condition assuming that information meant illumination when it was really nothing of the kind. But another thought came: Ernest was only halfway; there was a third step. Ernest had stopped swimming and his open mouth was pressed against the bowl, giving it a thick distorted appearance.

I said, "You have only gone halfway, you know."

Ernest's mouth opened a little wider with a slight gleam of dismay in his magnified eyes.

"Is there more?" he asked.

I smiled. "Much more."

In the silence that followed, Ernest and the bowl grew vaguer and vaguer and eventually faded away.

ERNEST DEPARTS

"Good Evening."

I had nearly completed the last few items in the Catalogue when I heard his greeting. This extension of my sense perceptions was somewhat upsetting, for it broke into my work and I felt I had more important matters before me.

I looked up.

Again the astral shelf and again Ernest swimming in his little glass bowl, and again another change in Ernest.

There was a bright light shining upon him, a gleam of astral sunshine that brought out little glints of gold from his scales; and he was much neater as though he had attended to his toilet; he also looked healthier. The ridiculous glasses had gone and he looked definitely a much more modest goldfish.

"Hello Ernest," I said. "So you are still about! How are you getting on?"

"Have been here all the time," he said somewhat dolefully. "Have greeted you but you never answered."

"Sorry Ernest, but I haven't seen you." It was difficult to explain to Ernest that as far as I was concerned he was only an astral mirage that had no true existence, but naturally I could not tell him so; though I must admit looking at him at that moment he was a very solid looking goldfish and the ripples he made in the water looked quite natural.

"Well—I 'er—you see—" I felt it difficult to reply.

Ernest did not wait. "I have read all your titles now, and have even managed to read some of the chapters

[*Catalogue and Review* (London: Atlantis Bookshop, 1947), p. 27.]

but"—here Ernest sighed and breathed a bubble—"I did not know there was so much; last time I spoke to you I thought I knew everything, but now there seems no end. There is more and more and more." As Ernest said this he went rapidly circling in the bowl. "If I know so much and still more of names and titles and chapters and places, what happens after?"

"What does happen after?" I mused; then a thought occurred. "Listen Ernest, after you have had so much information you feel limited, you want to get out, you have a lot of information but you feel that a good memory isn't sufficient; you are swimming about in a bowl and you see me outside and you want to get out of the bowl, but before you can do that you must change completely; now the same series of conditions applies to me: I live on a globe, you live in one and yet I am as much in prison in another sense as you are; we are all in prison and all the books and titles you have seen conceal various methods of getting out of prison. All I can suggest is to think and think and consider, and perhaps one day that light that is playing upon you and reflecting the gold that covers you will one day be reflected within you and then"—I paused—"and then you may discover a key to the mystery."

I looked at Ernest and the only way he could express his joy at the promise of the future was to swim round ever more rapidly until he became a gleam of gold and the bowl and the shelf faded out, but before he went I heard him say very faintly:

"Thank you; goodnight."

A PARABLE

There was once a devout Christian who believed Christ said a certain thing, and as he journeyed through life he came upon the brethren of a church who replied that the Lord had meant otherwise. So they indulged in argument, politely at first; for good people never quarrel —in the beginning. But later, because this good brother still believed that Christ did say a certain thing, they despaired for his soul and saw wickedness therein— though he was a Christian.

Therefore they said that his crooked thought needed straightening. They beheld small red flames burning within his being and saw that the Evil One had made a nest therein. So, unwillingly and with great sorrow in their hearts, and because he was unaccompanied by followers, they resolved to exorcise the Devil by putting their brother to the torture.

After long trials and preliminary rituals and much compassion—and also prayers—they began, with careful ceremony, the infliction of diverse methods of pain.

First they twisted his limbs—not in order to kill him, but to make him admit they were right and he was wrong. Yet he did not do so; on the contrary: he was exultant and fixed his mind upon Christ and gloried that he should suffer even as his Saviour had once suffered.

Then, as the acolytes sprinkled from impressive censers sweet incenses and chanted low-toned prayers, they inflicted numerous flesh-peeling upon his nude form until the smell of his own blood tasted saltily in his nostrils, and the perspiration from his pain diluted his

[*Occult Observer* (London), vol. 1, no. 1 (May 1949): pp. 31–39.]

welling blood. Yet he exulted exceedingly despite a few animal moans; for he still fixed his mind upon his Lord: the blessed Jesus Christ.

Thus his opponents were exceedingly grieved; for they saw that he was stubborn and would not admit his unrighteousness. So in that windy chamber of torment they prepared, with lamentations in their hearts and pity in their eyes, a third affliction.

And they placed his body of twisted limbs and many wounds within a harsh cradle of inflexible nails, and, with loving care, rocked him gently to and fro. This suffering hurt sorely; for, though it did not thrust his soul from his body, the nails discovered fresh portions of his frame untouched before. Yet still he was exultant; for his mind and heart were fixed upon the vision of his Saviour, Who had once died for him. And his tormentors heard feeble cries issuing from his mouth, and because they were low and faint they bent and listened and heard, in astonishment and wrath, that he did not recant his heresy; but sang in praise of his Lord.

So they cried: "Alas! he is still possessed of the Devil who must be driven forth."

Then in that gloomy vault of shadows and torchlights they lifted him from his cradle and laid him gently upon the freezing flagstones; for he was ill in mind and his body sadly exhausted. And with loving hands they placed the crucifix upon the ruins of his face; for much of it had been destroyed by the severe nails. And amid bitter sobbing, for the hearts of the cowled brethren were heavy with tears because the Devil had entered and had caused to stray the mind and soul of this brother, they prepared the fourth struggle for his salvation.

And they raised him upon an ingenious construction:

an instrument of wheels and ropes and strong knots, and into the dim hearing of this ecstatic lover of Christ rose the clang of massive metal and further hymns from the sad choir of this other church.

Then, with much panting and labour, they entwined the ropes about his ragged flesh and strove, with fixed purpose, to thwart the thing of evil that lurked obstinately within the crevices of his soul.

They pulled and they tugged and they groaned; but they strove in vain to drive out the sly ghost that dwelt within its victim. The dark arches of the vaults rang to the sounds of wheels and panting, yet lo! when they placed their ears to his parched mouth and shrivelled lips they heard thin cries of "Hallelujah."

So they despaired; for his soul had not yet come unto its heavenly kingdom. Then they ceased turning the wheels and pulling the ropes, and sat down and conferred. And afterwards they lifted the uneasy thing from its high place, and were, with great care, preparing the fifth torment; when, with a loud cry of "Hosannah," their fallen brother expired.

For the ties of his enraptured being were easily unloosed, and the filmy robes of his soul became wings upon which he sped, with great rejoicing, heavenwards.

Now his soul was filled with a sea of light; his imagination expanded like a tree with many fruits; the embroideries of his vision filled all space, for had he not died for his Lord? Had he not suffered four torments that were bewildering in their rich varieties of pain? And had he not withstood such assaults for the sake of his Redeemer?

Thus his spirit was glad-eyed, and the subtle elements of his being danced with deep joy about the boundaries of his senses. And he foresaw the jewelled throne upon which he would be seated; he heard the angels clap their hands and the organ of the stars welcome him with a new song in praise of his martyrdom. As he darted into the deeps of the Universe he imagined the tender fingers of the Lord clasping his and His shining face welcoming him with love; for had he not fallen about the battlements of his body to keep the light of his Lord's words aflame? Had he not fallen for His sake? Because of this would not a mansion be prepared for him of agate and onyx and silver and gold and ivory: a house of precious things?

Thus he rejoiced as his intangible substances plunged through many layers of celestial life; for his mind was fixed strongly upon his Lord and the gardens of the Universe could not tempt him to pause amid such eternal Edens for rest. In such wise did he reach the dwelling place of Christ.

Before the ornate gates of Heaven he stood; for they were closed, and high above he beheld, peering through the graciously curved bars, the countenances of many cherubs; as they fluttered and called with sweet voices the lambent feathers of their wings filled the serene air with soft flames, and he gazed in great pride at their delicate beauty; for were they not the servants of the Lord, and would not even He command them?

Now through the slim rods of crystal and lapis lazuli and rare metals he beheld a simply-clad man who walked in great dignity towards the gates; and he recognised this man as St. Peter; for he held a key that shone like a sceptre and was heavily encrusted with gems. And St. Peter nodded gravely and unsmilingly to him as he slid the key into the mysterious wards of the lock; for they were of Heavenly conception, and are not the least things made in Heaven possessed of beauty and wonder?

Now St. Peter greeted the exultant figure in low tones and chill words; so that the pilgrim felt that a frost had entered Paradise and blew coldly upon the rapture of his desires. And he looked up and saw that the eyes of St. Peter were harsh stars of angry grey. Then astonishment and dismay fell bleakly upon the spiritual essences of this wanderer and he waited humbly as the gate swung smoothly back and gave him freedom to enter.

In this wise did he enter Heaven; sorely puzzled and his exultation dropping from him like a falling fire.

Now as he trod the enchanted floor of Heaven—a floor of strange surfaces that was as a stream of smooth waters that gently sang, yet was also soft as down and yielding, and yet again as a benign sunlight brushed by the bloom of dusk—the chemistry of his substances distilled a heaviness within his limbs, so that they moved slowly and in fear; for he was sadly afraid.

He did not gaze at the trees of emerald and ruby and chrysoprase planted by the seeds of prayers, whereon the angels and cherubs could rest: for is it not known that the holy flocks of God have not, nor need, the physical counterparts of man? His eyes were humbly lowered and a perplexed foreboding bemused his mind. Had he not been violently translated for the sake of his Master? Yet the glad cry of trumpets did not sound in greeting. Neither did the hosts of the Lord aureole him in loud music. Nay, cold silence lay as a seal upon all Heaven.

Therefore he sighed and trod meekly after the figure of St. Peter: whose back showed disapproval. In this wise did he tread to the very house of the Lord: a noble habitation whence issued doleful harmonies and sometimes a quiet weeping. And here it was that St. Peter departed.

Before the intricately fashioned portals of the Lord's home he stood; the Hosannahs that had shouted in his heart now silent; the rich visions of his mind shrivelled up. His spirit had flown like a proud eagle; his soul had brought forth wings. Now both powers had passed away. Thus he stood and waited.

Then as he faced this shining door glazed with cunningly wrought enamels that was shaped like two wings that nestled one to the other, they unfolded and a voice, soft as a bell heard amid twilit hills, bade him enter. And in awe and joy and fear he trod over the thin threshold of woven blossoms; for the sad mystery that awaited his homecoming was about to be revealed to him.

Now before him ran a corridor of such light that he could not see the marvels inscribed upon its walls, and in his ears breathed the holy voice, beckoning him to his destined place. And as he trod with hesitant footsteps he heard a frail whispering: "Lo! he cometh. It is he; it is he." Then his fear grew and overclouded his awe and joy; for he did not understand, and the widespread draperies of his senses receded within him. Thus it was a small spirit that entered the holy chamber of our Lord.

Now a sore sight greeted him; for he beheld that within that noble place stood a most marvellous bed instead of a throne, and, resting within that bed, lay a very sick Man. His brows were damp with the thrust of some inward agony; the fingers of His shining hands were knotted as though in great pain; and the wells of His godlike eyes were aflame with some deeply rooted scourge.

And about Him stood austere archangels who chanted

magic words that fell as cooling flowers about the bed, and in the air small cherubs fluttered unhappily and uttered shrill and distressed cries. And the archangels made way for the small spirit that had entered; drew back in disdain as he approached the bedside. And a cherub darted down and hissed angrily into his ear as he knelt adoringly beside the bed; for he recognised that he worshipped the Lord Jesus Christ: Who again seemed crucified upon an unseen cross.

Now this was the greatest mystery of all; a mystery above all mysteries; a matter never recorded by the sages and saints of the Church. And daringly he ventured within the circle of the Lord's halo; for he heard sounds that gasped from the parched lips as though his Lord had fallen into a divine delirium. Yet the cries were familiar. As he hearkened, he remembered the sounds, remembered. . . . They were the same, these cries, as the cries he himself had uttered when afflicted by those diverse torments upon Earth.

THE DREAM TREE

When I was seven I had a remarkable dream; an experience that—child though I was—stood out with a strange shining vividness; and this dream would return again and again like a luminous memory of a place that I knew was not of this earth, and the sweetness and beauty and wonder of it would awaken such intense and utter longing that for days after I would fall into a deep melancholy; for this vision was of a fragrant place I could not enter at will; was remote and hidden in the misty territories of sleep.

Some hours before this dream I had greatly annoyed my foster-mother through having broken an ornament she valued and was sent to bed even earlier than usual. Having put out the light and taken away my favourite book, I cried myself to sleep. Then abruptly I was awake again; awake in the vital colouring of an unfamiliar countryside and I was standing before a door.

It was an ancient wooden door; green and worn and knotted; smooth and shining with a patina painted by great age. It beamed friendliness; like a personality who welcomed, and had always welcomed, the visitor. The lintels had curiously carved devices like mediaeval knights and giants and beasts, but only through the petals, delicate laves and tendrils garlanding these lintels could I see these small vignettes in the wood. Overhead, the porch glowed mellowly, enamelled with tones of colour, and from all these flowed exhilarating fragrances.

So I stood there; with keen longing, staring and

[*Occult Observer* (London), vol. 1, no. 1 (May 1949): pp. 51–55.]

waiting before this door in my dream, which was closed, and upon which I dared not rap; for there was neither knocker nor bell. And it seemed, after the burden of long, heavy hours that this door slowly opened to me. . . .

Even now, this dream of my childhood is unforgettable: the intensity of that moment when the door silently opened and a tall figure whose face—whether hidden beneath the fine light of purity or veil, I could not distinguish—stood shining down. Wonder and awe and a happy confusion eddied within me as her eyes smiled; eyes caressing and compassionate. Perhaps the small griefs of my daytime life were still reflected in my face, for she stooped—remember I was but seven —and lifted me up; and it seemed I was lost in a bewildering blaze of tender singing light, and she pressed me to her breast, and there was such sweetness that I no longer had self-being but was bathed in an unbearable vastness of weaving light. Then, gently, very tenderly, she set me down.

So I stood there, yet much of me still in her arms, and the blissful light still echoing and dimming away within me; it was as though I had been upon a great flight; now vaguely remembered, but without longing or uneasiness. Now I was content to stand there and wait. . . . Then in my dream she led me: through rooms barely remembered; the first being in shadow; but such brightness flowed through the window of the second room that I saw nothing else. Then into a garden we stepped.

To this day I can feel the firm, friendly clasp of this veiled woman—fingers smooth and of a sweet whiteness—gathered about my hand and leading me through this fragrant place. And I knew that the elements from which she was made were not human and that radiant qualities coursed through her. Light she was and her tread made no sound; likewise were her robes of a texture of an unfamiliar silver and golden shining that draped and folded about her; and she wore a girdle of dazzlingly enamelled doves cut from precious stones.

In this dream I walked as in a trance: without haste, without fear or doubt; with the certainty that what was to be revealed was exceedingly great; for in the distance I beheld a hill of light; its manifold brightness adding to the glitter of petals and translucent grasses. But as I gazed at this hill and neared it I saw it was a tree, but whether light emerged from this tree or the tree emerged from the light I could not discover; but I knew I was now entering a high place where all moments were great moments and—child though I was —I felt not only reverence but expected revelations. I was aware of deep imminent matters. Holy presences breathed in this garden and spread a tender anodyne of healing: comforting and caressing me.

Now amid the branches of this tree I beheld many fruits shaped like plums, yet richly coloured; some of burnished fiery gold, others opalescent blue with glints of scarlet in their depths, and others as swift silver veined with traceries of amber tendrils; and there were many to which I could give no name. But there was one fruit beyond all amid a caress of leaves and far beyond my childish reach that fascinated: of bluish jade and with an ardent fire breaking through its smooth haze and lighting the leaves about it. At this I stared, enchanted. Forgetting the gentle lady beside me. Even the light of the tree was less than the light of this fruit. Oh! to possess this! Thus did a new longing overwhelm me. Having entered this celestial garden another hunger now awoke.

Then the cool rich voice of the lady came to me; and there was laughter in her tones as well as a little sadness:

"It is not for eating, child, it is not ripe."

I turned to her, my small eager greedy hands clutching at her garments:

"Please, please," I cried. "It is so pretty, so pretty." My shyness had gone: I was all impulse and urgent pleading. The fruit filled my vision. "Give me it; give me it."

She laid her hand on my restless head, and a soothing sweetness drifted through me: "Listen child, the fruit is not yet ripe, but if you will do what I ask you, someday you will receive that fruit, but not yet. Now look higher, there, right to the top of the tree. Do you see it? A nest."

At first it was difficult; for though the tree did not have many branches the shimmer of light from twig and bough and leaf hid the top of the tree within a great haze. Yet as the lady pointed the nest became clearer, and like a lattice crystal basket it seemed to sway within a fragile clasp of leaves. To my smallness it was frighteningly high.

"Yes, I see it." Then again I turned to stare at the fruit. She stopped: "Now child I want you to do something for me. I want you to pick that fruit, but," she paused, 'but this will not be easy; I want you to climb with the fruit to the nest and place it in the nest."

I stared wonderingly at her: to climb the tree and pluck the fruit would not be difficult. I had climbed many trees, but to put fruit into a nest? This did not make sense. Eggs were in nests, not fruits.

So I stood in this bright dream within the dazzle of

this tree staring and puzzled till, most reluctantly, I obeyed.

Into this tender all-embracing glow I stepped and I glanced back at the veiled figure who stood beyond that fringe of light; but the golden haze suffused her in a tall dimness and a distance. Yet in that moment she was almost forgotten; for a child's interests are intense, but of short duration. I had now discovered a fresh delight: the tree called me with an attraction not to be denied. I placed my cheek against its cooling yet luminous bark; my small hands stretching and embracing it and the tree welcomed me: it was vibrant and lapped me in an enfolding light. Then, lightly and eagerly I began the ascent; my small fingers easily gripping the crevices in the bark; and though the trunk was high I soon reached an overhanging bough, and peering here and there, located the fruit.

Not all this dream is vivid, and from the moment I plucked the fruit and felt the tree quiver to the moment I reached the interlaced light that was the nest into which I gently placed the fruit, all was a happy trance.

And then—and then—from above there flashed a feathered rainbow; a darting harmony of hues—great bird eyes above a glaze of scintillating breast and amid the echo of golden gongs and a spindrift of perfume. I fell and floated; fell through and drifted down a funnel of darkness; fell and—awoke.

FROM AN UNFINISHED MS.

MAN AND HIS BEAST

A PARABLE

There was once a young man who wished to do good. Greatly compassionate because of the wickedness and confusion that flourished everywhere, and because the sins of the world weighed heavily on his heart, he read much, travelled far and meditated deeply. He visited the wise, who most willingly gave him what they believed would do much good—and in the dusky light of their understanding this was good advice—though rarely through practical experience. Ultimately he arrived in the marketplace of theories and idealisms, and among the many he met there were some who sold empty bowls and hollow vessels and who cried:

"If you would be pure repress your lower nature."

"If you would rise above your lower self kill out all desire."

"By starving the animal within it will become weaker and your higher nature stronger."

"Desire causes sorrow; it grows the sins of the world; therefore be as these empty vessels. Where there is no soil neither can there be fruits to feed appetites; and without appetites there is non-attachment."

"Desire drew you into birth; break from desire and you break from sorrow."

In such manner did they chatter and argue and quote, stroking their beards and looking solemn and wise. And they spoke about some who starved to death; about others who flogged their desires till their souls flickered over to the other side; and of others who through

[*Occult Observer* (London), vol. 1, no. 3 (1949): pp. 162–69.]

befuddled and sanctified stupidities were drawn to Nirvāna, until the young man believed that the death of all action meant liberation from sorrow and pain. Though he did not know that even compassion was desire and therefore some desires were noble. Yet it seemed paradoxical that the words *slay* and *kill* were so frequently used by those who bade him do good and avoid the infliction of pain upon even the lowliest of living things.

And after much meditation he considered: "I will drive desire from me; I will escape the manifold sorrows of existence; I will pluck my desires from me and become non-attached. Then shall I be free from all suffering."

Thus did he discuss these matters within himself, and thinking he was alone was astonished to receive a reply; a voice that rose to his mind in a mingled growl and purr, and thick as from a tongue unused to speech: "Master—I would speak to you."

The man asked: "Who are you?"

The voice replied: "I am the Beast within you who attends to your wants and appetites. I am the servant of your body, and Master—I have heard your thoughts; they are harsh and would oppress me."

And the man, who thought this voice was but imagined and so of slight importance, laughingly replied: "Why should I oppress you who calls himself Beast of my body and servant to my appetites?"

And the slow, thick voice replied: "O Master, I have been long with you and have sat at the table of your mind and know your counsels. There are some seated about the outer gates of your being who have told you to kill out desire; have told you appetites are perilous and pitfalls to your feet and that the illusions beyond our gates are evil snares to entangle your spiritual purposes. Master, I open the gates to the world and reveal the turmoil without, yet there is no evil in me; for do we not both enjoy pleasant things?"

And the Beast, encouraged by the silence of his Master, continued: "Now when you gaze into the heavens and you see constellations and planets, and the cosmic mists that hold the seed of stars, know this, O Master, that they are the mightier expressions of desire, when those who were once men became gods and planetary architects, building within the deeps of the universe their shining handiwork."

Now the voice of the Beast was as golden thunder beating against the ramparts of his Master's inner hearing: "If there was no desire there would be neither Heaven nor Hell; neither gods nor stars. Before you would destroy, comprehend the nature of your nature: that all parts have their great purposes, though the beginnings may be infinitesimally small, and that each has its place through the infinity of cycles. You are of immortal substance and I am thy faithful servant. Though many have cast me for a villain because I have appetites and hungers, through my senses you inhale fragrances and hear music; you bite into pleasant fruits and see colours."

The voice of the Beast dwindled; it was gentle, and purred; it drifted into stillness.

Then his Master replied, but because the Beast had spoken well and with vision he was confused; for he believed great truths had been spoken through the mouth of the Beast.

"You have spoken well, my servant, of heavenly designs

and the fruits of nature; you have bewitched my hearing with your tongue and waylaid my understanding; but the tribulations of the senses, the travails and temptations, that which lies in the dark of you, ready to rend my goodwill and understanding, you have veiled; hiding the heat and fevers of your heart, which glows and scorches and degrades when I would advance to loftier levels. No, I will kill out all desire; for as it has been said: 'All sufferings come from desire.' No—"

But the Beast interrupted hotly: "O foolish Master, how can you slay me? What trap can you use to snare me? I dwell in the den of your nature. I prowl through the roads of your being and hide in the undergrowth. Can you slay water? Can you maim the wind? If you oppose me, I will become terrible; I will enter into your slumber and into the garden of your mind; I will trample your dreams; I will break upon your peace and your works will be uneasy. Though I may not reach the throne of your spirit, I have much cunning, and I shall keep watch and spring through the secret gates and will howl in your mind. I will claw at the peace you seek and rend it into the rags of tumult; for I will become a Hound of Hell if you torment me. You cannot kill me, Master; let us dwell together in peace."

The man replied in despair: "How can we live in peace? Your habits eat at me, and when I would stand upright and go my higher way you bark at my heels; when I would give love, you breathe lust into me; and in my visions you appear with sharp teeth. No! Who are you to attack the sayings of the great sages who have said: 'Kill out desire and you slay pain and sorrow'?"

And the man thought: "At last I have silenced him;

for have I not shown I obey the noble precepts of the divine ones?"

Yet in the silence that followed the man sensed derisive laughter; for the Beast replied: "Surely the sage who had great compassion would never have used the words *slay* or *kill*. If he had reached great wisdom, he knew the nature of his nature; and that the Beast in him—who was also his faithful servant—was never slain, but raised up and ennobled; and worked with him in the wider field of compassion. Master, I believe a great truth has been twisted by those who followed but did not understand; for surely where there is no desire there is no movement, and no movement means death. And the compassionate who teach speak always of eternal life."

Now the Beast spoke gently: "Do you remember, Master, how friendly we were many lives ago? Do you recall the ancient days when you were strong and we worked as brothers, and life was rich and exciting? You did not oppress me but found me useful. Then you did not wish to slay nor torment me. I am but an animal, Master, but a good servant and have always been with you; though you never heard my voice I have spoken to you through your instinct and have warned you of dangers when we hunted through the jungle. Then I was helpful and you heeded me; your mind was young and your thoughts simple. Now I am your enemy, since you were told desire is evil; and you wish to murder me."

And his Master, who only wished to do good, had no reply; for he was perplexed. Many warnings had been given him by others who also wished to do good, yet were sickly and grim and barren and confused and obsessed with strong desires for health; who spoke of heaven, but most frantically desired to prolong their lives on earth; who meditated upon purity; who nibbled and nagged at their natures till their natures smote back and attacked their masters through devious and subterranean routes with disease and sickliness.

The inward voice continued: "Men call me beast, the animal in you. Others have made me a monster; they have tyrannised over me; they would make me small; they would trim my claws; they would cut off my limbs; they would make me toothless. Thus would they misuse my power and make me a weakling. Master, I would make a bargain with you. If you decide we must show enmity one to another, I will depart at once. I will leave your body and take with me my part of our inheritance. Goodbye, Master."

And the man rejoiced and did not reply but sat and meditated upon the Beast's decision, thinking: "If this Beast departs, I am free at last; the thorns of desire shall no longer prick me and there shall be peace within me."

In this manner did he commune and exult; dreaming of the future bliss within himself when he would be desireless and rise into the pure light of wisdom. "Now shall my understanding unfold. Now beyond confusion and the companionship of this Beast I shall dwell in the higher places of myself: the cathedral of my consciousness."

But as he exulted he heard a distant muttering and vague lamentations as from a hidden multitude. His inward eyes opened and he beheld happenings that made him ill at ease. Neither could he hold back the events into which he was falling.

For the lamenting multitude he heard, and who were leaving him, were the hidden servants of his servant. Now he knew that the Beast was drawing its inheritance from its dwelling-place and he knew too late that he had possessed much treasure. Now strength was pouring from him as from a broken vessel. Now he knew not only that the jewels and precious metals of his house had been mined by the Beast; but that the radiance within the jewels and the shining gleam from the metals came also from his wisdom. That the foundations of his dwelling had been erected by the Beast; but that he—the man—had brought in the lamps of understanding.

The small chatterings of his mind fluttered from him: gossips from the nest of memory twittering away into the incoming darkness—the flashing colours of a moment's ecstasy—delicate fabrics of sound and all that had enriched the intricate mansion of the man—these were drawn from him, following the departure of the Beast. Slowly the locks of his will fell apart. The feastings and the fastings were to be no more. The gathering darkness that was enfolding him hid neither secrets nor evil, neither virtues nor vice; all was diminishing.

And he thought: "So this is death."

And from the deeps of darkness came the voice of the Beast: feebly, sorrowfully: "No, Master, this is not death; this is extinction, non-activity; this is eternal nothingness."

Now his Master in great terror called: "Return to me, Beast, for I am afraid; for now I understand."

For now there was about the man a paralysing darkness, an abyss of nought, neither element nor desire; an utter oblivion to all his parts. And again he called to the Beast: "Return; return Beast and my servant; return, for the darkness and the void are too great for me to bear."

And in the voice of the Beast there was a cry of fear

and of joy: "Thy day was going from me, and the halls of our being falling apart; but now gladly will I return."

And his Master replied through the crevices of the darkness: "I was also afraid; but now I understand. Apart we are weak and dying, but together we are as metal."

And the Beast added: "Also our desires; we cannot kill our elements, nor can we dwell apart."

And as the Beast returned, the elements of the man, the firmament of his consciousness, were restored, and his house again filled with the small sounds of the minute servants of his servant, and all the senses again revelled in the dance of living; for the foundations of his mind were made strong again. And the man knew there would be sorrows and swift delights and the long, dull roads of living; but that his ethereal substance of the spirit and the metals of the Beast were eternal necessities.

So they returned and greeted each other. And the man knew that the many threads of his being were entangled in the threads of his hidden servant; and that neither could live and be aware without the other. And both knew they were immortal and eternal companions; that in some distant time the essences of the Beast would be purified. And the man knew that to be without desire meant extinction, and that a stupid misinterpretation was stupid in any age.

Then he heard the whisper of the Beast: "Master, Master, listen: I shall always be with you, and when you leave this body I shall follow you to the other side and still be your servant."

MURDER AND MYSTICISM

From the meadows of my own microcosm I plucked many blossoms, heavenly hued and delicately fragrant; purifying the senses and sweetening the human earth. Amid the ages I had gathered them into the great granary; reaping a spiritual harvest for the time when my nature reached ripeness and a great feast set before me in the evening of my illumination.

Overflowing with abundance was the soil of my nature; for the substances of my microcosm had brought nourishment and the little servants had given love: therefore all the parts were in gay accord and in graceful proportions.

But as I was seated there I beheld at the outer gates a lean and wolfish figure who spat and snarled and turned away and I asked: "Who is that man?" and was told he is an ascetic who carries the CEMETERY OF THE SELF.

I thought: "A strange phrase," and a grotesque vision of this man's actions appeared.

That he reigned over a barren land; that he was barbarian to his inner dominions, where the waters were a trickle and trees without fruit, where winters desolated amid cold winds. And I knew he was a sexton unto himself and a gravedigger: a self-assassin; for he wailed: "I must slay; I must kill; I must utterly destroy."

Therefore the shy green things did not grow, and the gentle forms could not browse, and the lilies had no ground for their roots.

Sadly I returned to my feast and he to his fast.

[*Occult Observer* (London), vol. 1, no. 5 (1950): p. 265.]

THE ADEPT AND THE IMP

> All the bright heavens still;
> All the harsh hells ashout.

"Look, Imp, up there." Belial spoke to his grinning servant, half-submerged in a muddy swamp, and pointed beyond the tormented crevices of roof: "There, see."

One long, crinkled and horny talon trembled at the unusually glittering light that—though shining from an immense distance—was so intense that Belial shaded his slanting eyes as he pointed.

The Imp looked up, then quickly down, for his sight was only accustomed to the sulphurous gloom and sky of tattered cloud, the bellow of thunderstorms and hurricanes. Yet he had seen the stately sapphire gleam and shuddered over its serene purity.

The Imp looked wonderingly at his master's malevolent green eyes and quavered: "Another task! what is the old —— brewing?" He inwardly cursed.

Belial smiled. There is no humour in Hell and Belial's smile was not light-hearted. The smile was a malicious grimace and the large green tusks parted and one talon thoughtfully scratched his black, leathery cheek. The smile hinted at secret infamies as he peered into the Imp's quivering face. "Imp," and his master's grin grew wider, "I want you to darken that light. I want you to destroy that light. It hurts my eyes."

"G-g-go up there? C-c-climb all the way? I-I am t-too small and i-i-it i-is far be-yond my powers," the Imp stammered.

[*Occult Observer* (London), vol. 1, no. 5 (1950): pp. 311–22.]

"Imp, that light is the light of an awakened man. Imp, with my knowledge that light can be extinguished through great temptations. You will go up there; he would recognise me at once for his eyes are keen and I bear certain signs. No, Imp, you will go and if you succeed I will give you many gifts, including—" he paused.

"Including—?" the Imp eagerly waited.

"The skin of his soul for your shoes," Belial snarled. "Now take this box of tricks and go."

Belial, who was exceedingly old and evil, knew the little and large corruptions; and whenever light flowered he would draw from his arsenal of evil that which would ruin and corrode and make barren that which might bring good to birth.

Now the green topaz glow of his eyes glared its hate as the light high overhead shone in love as he sent his would-be destroyer upwards.

Now Belial dealt in essentials: beauty, power, greed, lust, hate. Though all these were seldom needed for one victim; but he had overlooked one simple fact: this Adept had overcome all temptations, otherwise he would not have revealed his great light. Belial had attacked the incorruptible, and one small Imp could not scale such battlements.

He drew a deep breath, and the Imp, drawn into the magical hurricane of his powers, was blown upwards, spinning, rolling, tumbling upwards, tightly gripping a traveller's bag of tricks; up through brown mephitic mists; up to the place and radiance of the bright star.

*   *   *   *   *

Slowly the Adept awoke from his holy trance, the essences of his mind still fierily iridescent, the spire of his vision receding into a remote glory; the celestial carillons now a blur of sweetness as he descended back to man and earth. Yet a shining serenity was still within him as he opened his eyes to behold a suave stranger— immaculately clad—standing before him.

Belial, who knew the complete code of salesmanship, had missed no detail. Yet the Imp's bag of samples—though of bright polished hide—looked, somehow, unholy. To the discerning eyes of the Adept the materials, tanned in Hell, easily revealed their origin. And though the temptations were neatly packed they emanated a varied nastiness. The Imp, in a glint of black shoes and sharply creased trousers, looked, outwardly, spotless; but the Adept saw black hoofs, a black heart, and a small, sly face; possessing a sense of humour, however, he did not wish to disillusion this child from Hell.

The place of this meeting was on a high hillside overlooking deep, green valleys and great rivers; a rich perspective of nature in ripe abundance; an opulent panorama most refreshing to the eye, yet distant. Here the Imp could display his wares without interruption.

The Imp, blinking before the brightness of the Adept, imagined he was well hidden within his barrier of flesh, and introduced himself as a traveller who wished to present him with various samples.

The Adept smilingly returned the greeting: "You have something to sell?"

"N-n-not to s-s-sell, sir, b-b-but gifts." The radiance of this man was bewildering and made him uncomfortable.

"Gifts!" The Adept sounded pleased. "You are most kind, really kind!"

"B-b-but not from me," the Imp stammered. He did

not intend to share any blame if the plot went wrong. "A friend sent me."

"A friend," the Adept mused benignly. "Does he know me, and where are these gifts?"

"Here." The Imp pointed to his case. He was feeling more at ease. This enemy looked a thoroughly simple man, an innocent one too; kindly eyes and gentle smile. The case of magical tricks would overwhelm this shining fool. He would begin with the small temptations. His crooked soul grinned; he even foresaw the problem of transportation after this saint fell. This was his first big assignment. Absurd of Belial to give him so large a bag. One or probably two temptations would have sufficed.

Now the subject of magic is frequently a matter of glamour, and this bag held bottles containing essences, venoms, distillations of enchantments, spells, elixirs, narcotics for the imagination, herbs from Hell that could produce false Heavens; in short all substances to poison heart and mind and add to Hell's population.

The Imp opened a bottle of Vanity: an essence spreading sounds of flattery; voices acclaiming the Adept as the holiest of men, one loud voice leading:

"Ah! celestial magnificence, we the countless multitude acclaim you God of God. Command and we obey, all-wise and all perfect." And from minute voices in blades of grass, grave sounds from the distant boughs, from the baritone of falling waters, from the bells of a distant mountain-herd, even from the mountain itself and one small shining cloud that drifted by, came praise.

And the Adept listened and smiled, till the Imp thought: "What a simpleton!" then aloud: "I can hear all praise you, saint of saints; the world praises you; for your greatness dazzles them."

But the Adept was laughing loudly. "No, my friend,

I hear hollow echoes and a great braying. The hypocrisy of the world in a small bottle! Is this a gift from your friend?"

And the Imp, scowling in his heart and now uneasy, watched the Adept wave his hand and disperse the flatteries.

"An experiment, your holiness!"

"Somewhat childish," the Adept replied.

"I have other gifts."

Now the Imp released from bottle after bottle the little temptations: False Humility, to turn the Adept into a hypocrite; Greed, to bloat the flesh and degenerate the mind; vapours, to distort the vision; monsters ascending from the valleys, and mirages from the heights; all to bewilder and confuse.

And the Adept smiled in his calm fashion, and the temptations were not.

Now desperation convulsed the Imp; he had spread a festival of temptations—every dish of a hellish excellence—so well-spiced and tasty that any small nature would have smacked its lips and indulged in gluttony. Only in the last resort was he permitted to use the greatest temptation that would probe and weaken this contemptible and incorruptible one; this—and revolting images streamed obscenely through his emotions. If he could, if he dared? He gave a sudden yelp of anguish. Belial—who was below and watchful—tugged magically at his most sensitive portions.

The Adept, who knew the plot and the play, nodded sympathetically: "In pain?" he questioned. "Can I help you?"

The Imp shuddered. He came to corrupt, not to be cured. Belial would degrade him to the lowest Hell.

"Just a twinge," his writhing face croaked.

"This air is excellent for health." The Adept was most friendly.

The scenery was adrift in a golden and silver haze. Over the flocculent cloud of forest came the sudden winged rainbows of birds. In the exhilarating purity of this place the murmuring from below emphasised the profound gulfs between this illuminated man and the interests of the world. But amid these gentle sounds came the clear, thin notes of a bell, and the holy man was amused to see the ears of this dapper traveller from Hell twitch before these chimes.

The Imp's thoughts now wandered: his task was more difficult than he had expected. The pure light was unbearable to his senses; it dazed the murk in him; the screech and howling of his homeland were missing; this peacefulness painfully stroked and stitched at the rags of his character. "Belial, the dirty —— " he winced. Belial was in constant touch. He stared wildly into the kindly eyes of his victim.

"I have brought a friend."

"A friend?"

"A lady friend," the Imp explained. "She is behind that rock. Shall I bring her?"

"Certainly."

Now, proudly leering, his strut shouting "Victory!" he introduced Belial's masterpiece. Bewilderingly, delicately lovely; her draperies moon-misty; her great dove-gentle eyes imploring compassion and tenderness: she was silvery fair; lithe as a new lily. Her hair diaphanous aureole, tendrilled. Her slim hands, modestly folded, shone through a coif of light; her palely smooth feet trod as twin fluttering petals. She looked nun-like, subtly holy; formed from ethereal elements. Adoring devotee for an anchorite; but her fragrance was intriguingly cold, sweetly corrupt. This was the one fault in Belial's bewitchment; the seal of his satanic nature.

Now as she swayed there, cool and shimmering, her witch-heart brewing elusive snares; pale eyelids veiling mischief, the Adept looked so admiringly at her that the Imp inwardly roared. "At last!" and he recalled Belial's tales about desert hermits and men of God; for it had been an accepted tradition that holy men were celibate and succubae were zealously trained for their downfall. The Imp had been reared upon primitive and mediaeval legends; how their hair-shirts so irritated them that nymph-white limbs invariably brought them to Belial's sulphurous lakes—where they still hunted these elusive forms amid the gloomy mists.

The Adept turned to him, reproof in his tones: "Young man, I do not know by what magic you brought her here, but she is very lovely and should be protected."

"The old fox," the Imp inwardly grinned, and he heard the remote laughter of his master echoing. "I would most willingly leave her in your holy care," the Imp solemnly replied; "she will serve you and pray with you in your devotions."

"No, she will be a companion to my wife," the Adept explained.

"Wife!" Belial's assistant gasped. Outrage and alarm blended in his voice. The Imp was shocked. This man was unholy, a transgressor; openly revealing his necessity for a mate.

The Adept called: "My love, we have visitors."

Never before had the Imp beheld so much beauty as in this woman who now approached. The silvery sorcery of Belial's witch was eclipsed before the warm, golden sweetness of the Adept's wife. Here was no cunning elusiveness, no wantoning trap that slyly clawed, but harmonious proportions, gentle strength and aliveness; her bearing gave her simple dress queenliness; her glances caressed like her warm, low voice and the atmosphere quickened into an indefinable peacefulness; the lustrous shimmer of her hair was seen by the Imp as a soothing gold; her kind, blue eyes broke through the veil of his cunning and he trembled before the unconscious magic of purity.

Now the troubled mind of the Imp searched for the corruptible in this woman; for it was well-known in Hell that the weaker sex corroded good character; that woman turned the meandering stream of man's nature into a raging torrent and his sleeping passions into a hurricane through the gentle meadows of the mind; but the warm love this woman sent forth was all-embracing and endearing, and there was laughter in her wise eyes. Then the Imp sensed the complete understanding between the Adept and his wife and knew he had again failed as she led the succuba mincingly into the house.

And Belial, who observed this, broke into a palsy of rage till his tusks clicked and a sulphurous foam dripped hissingly upon the oozy floor.

"My queen succuba a slut for a kitchen!" he bellowed. "Imp," he commanded, "the greatest of all temptations, and *if you fail*—!" Through the turbulent cloud of rage whence spluttered his master's voice, the Imp received the message. He was to offer this holy man the world. Which meant foolish idealism governing for a short time and his master eventually acquiring an exceedingly strong slave.

Now this was to be truly big magic; to create a glamour, a comprehensive enchantment, till the victim yielded. He was to offer a planet with all its complex activities and the victim was to be tempted in all his weaknesses. Now the attack was to be multiplied a millionfold; these illusions would riddle the adamant of this man until all would collapse; until his egotism would be bloated and his appetites roar like a great fire.

The Imp now spoke fast and glibly. He hoped this temptation would sweep the Adept off his feet.

"My most expensive and exclusive sample. In here are the ingredients of the world, and by a subtle device these elements will give you control over every dominion, every force of nature, over every atom of this world and all the mechanics to use them. Here, take it.... No. Just watch me, sir; I will first demonstrate some of the powers such as key to earthquakes, volcanoes and all the catastrophes...."

"A most unpleasant bottle!" the Adept cried, and stopped the Imp from uncorking the phial.

The Imp stared, then realised that his eagerness had revealed his true intentions. He trembled. What would Belial do to him?

"If only in the power of the evilly intentioned. But in possession of th-the g-g-good!" He stumbled over this word as though it were an obstacle to his vocal cords. "In your hands, sir, all would be well. No disease, no misery, no wars, no death." He paused.

"And no life," the Adept added. "Changelessness is as bad as chaos."

"But, most honoured sir, think: you could change the destinies of every creature; you could possess every treasure; you could become Emperor of the World. Worship and applause from every tongue. Obedience from all beasts; reins to guide the winds; your kind purposes rule deeps and heights."

The Imp grew eloquent; he was no longer a commercial traveller from Hell but picturing his own ambitions; though cunningly hiding his sharp teeth beneath his gentle words. "Great multitudes under your control."

"Stop!" the Adept cried. "Enough! The bubble of power does not interest me; such thrones are thorns, and such crowns corrupt. Your bag contains strange samples; your wares have the smell of sulphur."

"And can your master give all this world to me, and is it his to give?" the Adept questioned. "It is a great deal; and all to me?" He nodded his head and solemnly repeated: "It is a great deal."

The Imp laughed complacently: "Sir, my master is a generous man."

"But," the Adept anxiously asked, "has he acquired all of this honestly?"

The Imp winced, then in a flash of evil wisdom replied: "Sir, he gained all this through thieves, yet honestly."

And the Adept, who appreciated the subtlety, sadly whispered: "Alas, few men live beyond the Devil's clutch." Then, aloud: "Would you also make me a thief? I will now reveal to you a little of my magic, for you have offered me power, love, flattery." He pointed below: "And all that."

So in this high place, where cool winds brought offerings of fragrance and gentle murmurings from a busy world, the Adept challenged Belial through his Imp.

And now, almost beyond the Imp's eye-reach, shone twin benign suns with blue impenetrable deeps set within a countenance filling all sky, and to his ears the measured pulse of a mountainous drum and torrential sounds of hidden streams; then the vision became an all-dazzling nimbus; then formed foaming into meteor blaze and his hysterical senses tumbling through abysses. The black, craggy bit of him whirling about vast incandescences, only the basalt of his being invulnerable: unyielding to this light. Form vanished into golden space: a heaven of gyrating stars: unfamiliar galaxies, coruscating, uncountable.

Now lightly he drifted, beyond Belial's aid—a small, scared Imp, his minute cunning forgotten, his little magic blown apart by this greater magic; scattered through a secret cosmos where haloes fiercely flared, and, above, the intense shining of a sun.

Now the drumming and the many sounds dwindled to murmuring and a hush entered these heavens; for the Adept was in paradisal meditation and into the dominion of his being came a great peace; his mind was ascending areas of bright wisdom and the Imp somersaulting amid a cataract of glory, for the Adept breathed celestial nectar and the cosmos sang hymns of welcome; anthems in praise of the unity of God. But all the bewildered sprite heard was a melodious thunder tormenting his distorted particles and he saw a brilliant light. Yet the virtues and essences of this purified cosmos could not sublimate this carbonised midge, and he wailed amid these lambent symphonic spaces for his master Belial; but his master could not hear; for the gulf between had become holy and all Belial's cunning could not solve the mystery of his servant's disappearance.

Meanwhile, the crescendo of peace had attained its perfect equilibrium; all notes were one golden crystalline chord moving in slow, royal sweetness; each star a gentle gong for this sonorous power; and there came the distillations from all fragrances into one royal fragrance;

till all ether was glorified, and the Imp was but a drifting cinder in boundless light, a pitiful black ash whose temptations had diminished to their true proportions, still gripping his traveller's bag of enchantments, lost in the cosmic empire of the Adept.

Now in this transcendent bliss of unutterable good, where all was poise and exaltation, this child of Belial beheld the activities of wisdom; for the Adept meditated upon purpose and the grinding out of good; its radiance flowering before the Imp's astonished gaze.

Through the luminous empyrean emerged a celestial architecture: prismatic girders threading constellations, riveted to the auras of stars and suns; cosmic mathematics and the scaffolding of universal principles that harmonised all into a divine unity from the remotest corners of these heavens. He beheld imperious buttresses and arcs lost in the infinite spaces. He beheld the spinning of microcosmic designs through the loom of consciousness. He beheld such riches that the temptations of his master became the trash of a beggar's gathering. He beheld the table of a cosmic banquet; he beheld the vessels and cups bubbling with the elixirs of supernal wisdoms and the shimmering fruits of accomplishment.

And this cosmic kingliness so dazzled the eyes of this poor Imp that he became blinded and, groping, he discovered a firmness beneath his feet, and all ethereal enchantments had vanished, and he again beheld the still figure of the Adept.

Then the holy man opened his eyes and smiled at the distracted little traveller; his clothes were disarrayed, his face dismayed; his sample case of magic was fallen from his nerveless hand and the trumpery spells scattered before the Adept's feet.

"I believe you were going to sell me something? Ah! I remember: the world and all its rich and varied possessions; its pomp and its poverty; its busy inhabitants and its fruits, had I accepted the dividends in terms of numerous powers; the lease as long as I did not oppose your master. And all—"he paused and smiled, "given in friendship. And what happened to those who did accept?"

There was no reply. Only an odour of sulphur revealed the small traveller's disappearance.

*   *   *   *   *

Belial glared at his quivering servant. The vortex of incident through which he had passed had—to the discerning eye of Belial—almost straightened the distortions of his slave. He glanced at the suitcase and its crumpled spells that followed the descent of the Imp, now floating untidily upon the surface of the muddy pool wherein the Imp had only recently wallowed.

"You're warped; hopelessly warped," he yelled, and hurled the poor wretch down the deepest abyss of Hell.

TRYST WITH LILITH

During John's wanderings through the inner worlds he lands, with his companions, upon a strange island; and after some astonishing incidents, he hides within a glen, and there emerges a beautiful figure of a woman.

"John," and the mystery and music she wove into my name, compelled me to respond; for there was a warring within me: one part all melting and entreating and longing; the other impassive, aloof, unwelcoming; yet her bewitchments crept into the very crevices of my nature. Now there was a lilt in her whisperings; her words were little waves that lapped about me; endearing, flickering words, and her arms about me:

> *There are briars about your love:*
> *Oh! let me break through the golden thickets.*
> *I will entwine you to me in the branches of my love,*
> *With the sweetness of all fruits, in the fragrances of all*
> *   flowers.*

And now I was neither youth nor man; nor was there haste or slowness, but only an ever enduring. I was no longer John, wanderer in strange lands; but all entranced emotion, all bewilderment, staring into the eyes as into an abyss.

"Who are you?" I whispered. "How do you know my name?"

"I am Lilith, and I have waited, waited." Her voice

[*Occult Observer* (London), vol. I, no. 5 (1950): pp. 328–30.]

was a rustle of leaves; she spoke as though words were unfamiliar.

"I am Lilith and I have waited. I am no enemy; are leaves, gentle petals, cool dews, the healing herb your enemies?"

Beneath a drift of fragrance and canopy of blossom I gazed into her large, green eyes—green eyes of a fawn but with the glow of wisdom. And though no woman had come into my life, her caressings were a shimmer of tenderness and passionate supplication to all my being; I knew she was not human, yet one part of me recognised the richness of a great love.

And though she was as a green shining about me, just beyond the ranges of memory, in tales and fables lay the debris, the hurt of poignant idylls, the rusting swords of failure, the utter weariness of the forlorn quest and armoured figures vanishing into the dusk of haunted woods, the melancholy of autumns, the drift of haggard leaves and the faded hues of ragged pennons. Such sorrowful memories brooded in me that I broke from her gentle clinging. Fragments from the tale of Undine, of the Lorelei, of nymphs; wraiths of sorrowful folklore and loves entangled amid enchantments: half-hidden faces and imploring eyes swirled through barriers within me of which I had been unaware.

"They would rescue others but could not rescue themselves; pride and conceit and arrogance defeated them." She pleaded as I would go from her: "Why be afraid because I see with your eyes and know the hurt of your heart? Why fear me?"

Her fingers wove into mine; their cool vibrancy drawing at my hesitations, the green irises of her eyes drawing me back; then she smiled. And I knew. Here was no witchcraft, no reticent slyness. Here was Nature in sweet revelation.

All the green soothing, green cleansing, through latticing leaves, drift of dove-grey light and beneath the lave-lovering of glances. Ah! suppliant, pliant Lilith; Lilith, the ever-changing, unchanging! Mingled sweet of the green, the gold, the delicate dark. Tendering fingers and mouth, all Maytime's voice and breasts of April's sap; eyes soft emerald . . . . Your voice: the croon of leaves, hill-high, with hints and glittering of secret wisdoms; the governing and ordinances of hidden ways . . . . Yet I knew you not; for you were white limbs and over-crowning hair and green veilings, of fragile caressing and fine fire, subtle weavings of tender fingers, greenily cool in the silvered air. All senses rewoven, emotions woven through looms of living, small ecstasies banqueting; all my being dedicated, the gay toys of my imagination entangled in this green delirium who was named Lilith, who was enchantress: whose voice was a silver nocturne, who awakened all my elements amid welcoming intangibles . . . .

FROM A MS.

THE THREE CENTAURS

John, who is narrating this tale, to seek the Crystal City
must journey through the perilous jungle. He has met the
gods Dionysus, Athena and Jupiter. He has been given an
immortal flower and escaped the menaces of the City of the
Great Voice and its factory of Mechanical Unity. Now,
alone and defenceless, and some little way in the jungle,
he comes upon three grotesque creatures within a glade.

They were caricatures of figures strangely familiar,
and as I stared—their names eluding me—I suddenly
knew: Centaurs. They were as those of Greek origin
but smaller; the tallest was level to my shoulders. The
Donkey Centaurs were three: one a young female. The
eldest had a grey, straggling beard, dark angular features
and wore thickly-lensed spectacles. A black frock-coat
spread towards his rump and long tail, and he wore two
pairs of short trousers—wrinkled and baggy—that came
a little below his knees, revealing four small, muddy
hoofs. His beard concealed his throat, but the lower
buttons of a stained waistcoat were unfastened. Slung
across his body was a strap supporting a specimen-case.
His voice was pompous and booming.

The female was smaller and wore a two-piece cos-
tume, dark and creased; the jacket somewhat masculine
in cut and a stiff white collar about her small throat. Her
face was pointed and sallow with bright anxious eyes
and her brown hair was gathered loosely in a bun. Her
arms were bare and bony and her nimble, thin fingers

[*Occult Observer* (London), vol. 1, no. 6 (1950): pp. 375–85.]

picked from the grass small insects which she popped into her specimen-case.

The third was a young, male Centaur with a long, solemn, fair face and snub nose supporting large glasses. A thin jutting chin and thin mouth gave him an expression of great determination. His fair hair was neatly brushed, but his left cheek constantly broke into a spasmodic palsy which he would absent-mindedly slap into stillness.

As I watched this amazing trio, the female Centaur suddenly saw me:

"Look, look: a young anthropoid!"

I stepped into the glade. I had assumed the undergrowth had hidden me; now concealment was unnecessary, and these creatures looked harmless enough.

"Good morning." I could think of no other manner to greet them.

"Good morning to you," they replied.

"Where are you going, young anthropoid, and why are you here?" the bearded Centaur questioned; then, before I could reply, "but first—introductions. My name is Dr. Achilles Wallow, and these," pointing to his companions, "are Miss Hermione Follow and Mister Hector Hollow, my pupils in psychological research and, as you can perceive, fully occupied. Now to return to my original question: What brings you here and where are you going?"

Again the questions "why" and "where." I did not know how to begin, though I tried: "I came through a door, a secret door—and then—and then I found myself on the other side. Then I met—" I paused. This was no time to give details. "Someone who told me I would meet a friend after I journeyed through this jungle. He would take me to the Crystal City." I stopped.

They had been listening intently until I mentioned the Crystal City.

"Rubbish," the doctor snorted. Hermione tittered and Hector guffawingly brayed.

"The mythological mixture as before," the doctor sneered, then turned to his grinning pupils. "What is the formula?"

Both spread their forelegs apart, bowed till their noses touched the grass, raised their heads and chanted:

"Mud came before mind and death to moonshine."

"Precisely," the doctor boomed. "Precisely. Mud came before mind and death to moonshine." He looked severely at me. "Young anthropoid, though you have come from the City of the Great Voice, originally we all come from here—the jungle, and there is no hidden door nor is there a Crystal City: they are the vestigial fragments of primitive anthropoidal vision. You have, of course, spoken to the gods?" He smiled patronisingly.

"Yes," I replied impulsively, "Dionysus, Athena, Jupiter—"

"Enough, enough," he interrupted. "The yeast of your mind has turned into Haemorrhagia Mythologica or Fantastic Fabulae." He turned to his students: "These are new terms; please record them."

I was angry now. The steamy growths and sour-sweet smells of corruption no longer made me uneasy; for upon meeting these creatures the evils and perils of this jungle were temporarily forgotten. How dare they deny me my experiences; how dare they laugh at me! Surely the lapel of my coat revealed glittering proof, a cool blaze of petals Dionysus had given me?

"Look," I pointed dramatically at the flower.

"That, my dear anthropoid, is a flower which we observed when you first appeared. Well?"

"This was given me by Dionysus!" I shouted.

"Don't be foolish, anthropoid. Just imagination. You wish to embellish your ego; you wish to be noticed, so you decorate yourself. A Nature Neurosis." He turned to his pupils. "Record this as well: Nature Neuroses." He smugly stroked his beard as his pupils admiringly cried:

"A pun, doctor, a pun! Neuroses, new roses."

Hermione sniffed: "Anthropoids are nasty creatures, all criss-cross and uncouth. All croth-crith and untooth. All crooth-cruth and untruth. All—" She was becoming incoherent and began to choke, her eyes glassy. Hector, who apparently knew these symptoms, padded up to her, and placed his hand across her mouth until she stopped.

"More control, Hermione, more control," the doctor called. "You may call him young Anthropoid Incomplexicus."

"My name is John Witless," I shouted, "and you are only donkeys with human heads." At that moment I saw nothing amusing about my situation.

This incident was interrupted by Hector Hollow, who was behaving in a curious manner. He became rigid, his head aslant, one arm outstretched and immoveable. "Do not come near me," he warned, "I am a perfume bottle of the most expensive kind." He sniffed ecstatically and the sheer beatific silliness of his expression made me laugh outright. "I smell beautifully," he beamed.

Dr. Wallow made notes. "The sixth transference within two hours," he proudly remarked; then explained: "Hector is very sensitive and can imitate many of our patients."

"And does this go on all day?" I asked.

"Hector can imitate any patient," he replied.

"Hector cannot help it," Hermione added.

But Hector was no longer a scent bottle. The transference had left him and he moved about as though nothing had occurred. Then Hermione called: "Doctor, doctor, you are doing it again."

I also watched in amazement as the doctor began to tie his beard to his tail which was long and easily reached it, but he had already stopped when his pupils recalled him from an apparently absent-minded act.

"H-m-mm, h-mm-m, erh-mm," he grunted. "Forgetfulness, just forgetfulness. I feel that a short explanation to our young anthropoid about his condition will be of great advantage to him. Now every anthropoid is ill. This is the first great principle laid down after centuries of research. Every anthropoid is ill." He paused: "Why?" Again he paused. "They are ill because they are wrongly shaped. In their efforts to stand upright they subjected their anatomies to abnormal stresses, to pressures in wrong places; subjected them to their ambitions to pluck fruits from the highest branches."

"But that is the giraffe, doctor," Hector interrupted.

The doctor stared angrily at his pupil. "Mister Hollow, both have attempted to stand upright." He turned to me: "Do you like fruit?"

"Naturally," I replied.

"Naturally: did you hear him say so?" Then pompously: "It is the nature of the anthropoid to attempt the impossible, and the burden of standing upright drives him into absurd directions leading to such ailments as the Myth Sickness, the Superiority Overflow, the Phoenix Sacrifice."

"Or fry your eggs then hatch them," Hector jeered.

"All immortality fixations, over-decorated and buried beneath flamboyant imageries, can be simplified into one great fear: refusal to return home. Anthropoids, being naturally diseased, make desperate attempts to escape from their unhappy states. Thus the history of these poor creatures—" he paused and patronisingly stared at me—"reveal efforts to build systems and philosophies, religions and strange heavens for their comfort—and to move away from their ancestral memories, which are here, to non-existent Utopias, fabulous places —the anthropoidal Schema Mythologicum. Ill at ease in his anatomical deformities, his conceits stronger than his reasoning, intoxicated by the noxious fumes of ill-health, he chases his hallucinations and believes them to be as real as this jungle .... All this," again he paused, "is utter nonsense."

"Yes," I shouted, "utter nonsense."

Hector and Hermione, who were writing this lecture in their notebooks, looked up in surprise at my interruption.

"The young anthropoid agrees with the doctor," Hermione shrilled.

"But I do not agree!"I shouted.

"You said what the doctor said," they accused.

I shrugged my shoulders over this absurd argument and listened to the doctor rambling on.

"... And this desire to be superior makes outrageous demands upon his animal appetites, for his true heavenly state is to be completely unrepressed, like ourselves. Personally speaking, and without offence, we think you are harmless monsters. Besides, perfection is not for all, and there are few like us," he smirkingly concluded. But he was not ended, and pointing at the savage surroundings: "Look, all of these growths are uninhibited,"

228

he said, "they grow as they please, and are the free expressions of Nature. All anthropoids should be in a similar condition, and our researches attempt to uninhibit the repressed anthropoid."

Again he reached for his tail, but was stopped by his pupils.

So intently had I been listening to the doctor that I did not notice what Hermione was doing until I heard the rattle of a falling specimen-tin and turned to see the creature trying to climb a tree. She had already reached the higher branches before one had snapped and sent her tumbling.

"Hermione is always trying to climb trees," explained the doctor. "She tried to fly once. Said she was Pegasus."

Hector and I ran to pick her up, but she was unhurt and began gathering in the various repulsive insects that were creeping from the opened specimen-tin. This she did without a shudder, and I was amazed at her indifference.

The doctor looked musingly at me, then turned to his pupils: "Students, what is the disease of this young anthropoid?"

"I am not ill," I retorted.

Miss Follow ran round me crying: "He is a tree! Stand still; stand still and you will soon be an orchard." The others joined her dancing round me, Hollow's voice echoing: "An orchard, an orchard!"

They were serious; neither smile nor flicker was on their faces as they chorused this nonsense.

"But I am not a tree; I do not wish to be a tree, and all this is ridiculous," I laughed.

"What, not a tree?" They sounded astonished. "The other patient wanted to be one."

"But I am not a patient!" I argued.

"You must be and we will cure you. I tell you all anthropoids are ill, so you must be a patient!" The doctor panted, then stopped; the others did likewise.

Hector's cheek rushed into another spasm. Again the doctor absent-mindedly tied his tail to his beard before his pupils could stop him, and Hermione tried to walk on her hind legs—though with difficulty, her skirts falling away and revealing a curious jumble of underwear over which she stumbled and fell backwards. The doctor could not help her as he was disentangling himself, and Hector was motionless as though listening.

I heard it too—a monstrous grunt, and terrifyingly near.

Now these Centaurs and investigators into life in the raw and primitive did not wait to investigate and analyse. Neither did I. The doctor, in his efforts to disentangle himself, ran in feverish circles, but his delay was brief. I followed Hector and Hermione into the darkest and densest part of the undergrowth. Here the grasses sloped into a twilit cavern of roots: moist and unhealthily close, but bringing a sense of security. Here we huddled and listened.

"It sounded dreadfully near," Hermione panted.

"What was it?" I whispered.

If these inhabitants were afraid, how should I feel? Fears I had before entering the jungle returned. I shuddered and felt sick.

"No one has ever seen it," the doctor replied, "only heard it."

"Because we have always hidden ourselves," Hermione explained.

"But there have been tales," Hector added. "It is too big to be destroyed; much too big."

In this leafy refuge their little pomposities had vanished; now they were small creatures comforting one another.

"They say it lives in an abyss across the river." Hermione's voice was dry and her eyes apprehensively bright. Her pointed face quivered as she nervously tidied herself.

"The most monstrous and biggest beast in the jungle," said the doctor.

"And utterly uninhibited," said Hector.

"And therefore the most perfect," I suggested. Why I made this remark I was uncertain; but it did sound reasonable.

"There are limits, young anthropoid," boomed the doctor peevishly.

"But surely not in perfection?" I persisted. I had irritated him and felt justified. Had he not jeered at and patronised my species, suggesting we were all diseased? I had but carried his philosophy further, and if the doctor's idea was complete lawlessness—and the jungle surely expressed this—then the beast was obviously the jungle's finest expression. Nevertheless, I was greatly afraid; for I remembered my visions of the abyss and the challenge from the beast in the dawn.

Hector was now peering through crevices in the leaves and called: "I think it has gone, doctor."

The doctor, who had not replied to my argument, seemed pleased at this interruption: "It is so huge," he said, "that we receive ample warning, and we have not heard it for quite a time."

"When the last anthropoid visited us, doctor," Hermione reminded him. "Do you remember?"

"Ah yes, the one upon whom we endeavoured to

operate," the doctor agreed. "A stupid anthropoid; dreadfully tangled mind—deplorably obstinate. Said he did not wish to be improved. Called us donkeys. We, who have descended from the Centaurs!"

"You mean ascended," Hector reminded him.

"Of course, of course." The doctor nodded.

"That anthropoid broke the Dream Disintegrator," Hermione recalled.

"And the Neuroses Thresher," brayed Hector.

"Also he disconnected the pipes of the Great Dis coordinator," concluded the doctor.

"He must have been fierce!" I said.

"Fierce!" the doctor's deep voice became slightly falsetto: "Fierce! He was ruthless. He savaged me, punched Hector and slapped Hermione. He was in a most translucent state."

"You mean truculent?" I suggested.

"Young anthropoid, the words I use are precise. Each term has been distilled through retorts and test-tubes; they have undergone the uttermost pressures till their exact proportions have been calculated. I said *translucent*, meaning the mind in a 'clear gaseous condition possessing only a slight chemical content.' An anthropoidal condition of no use whatsoever: visionary, undefinable, almost invisible."

Whilst he was explaining these matters, we were already back in the glade, and Hermione and Hector were gathering their scattered specimen-cases, ready to depart.

I stood watching, bewildered, unable to reply to the doctor's explanations and undecided about my journey.

"You are of course coming with us," the doctor called. The others had already disappeared through the narrow pathway. "We are returning to the Academy."

"An academy, here, in this jungle?" I questioned in surprise.

"And where else? Naturally in this jungle. An academy for all psychological ailments, abnormalities, obsessions, repressions, split personalities. Here we refit and recondition the most extreme cases sent to us from the City of the Great Voice."

"And then you return them to the factory of the Mechanical Unity," I added.

"Yes; so you have been there?"

"I visited it, though not as a patient," I explained. Again I felt uneasy. Apparently these creatures also operated; though they spoke and acted so absurdly that they seemed quite harmless. "You see I did not need any operation as I feel quite healthy."

"Young anthropoid, I am glad to hear this. The jungle is the home of your ancestors, and you should feel happiness and contentment here. A completely freed anthropoid—"

"But I do not feel safe here and I certainly have no wish to live here," I explained.

The doctor looked sadly at me: "All the elements of the jungle are woven through you; you cannot discard its memories."

I no longer argued. I had no desire to be alone in this jungle and these fantastic creatures were well-meaning. Also, my curiosity overcame my fears. A school for mental diseases administered by donkey Centaurs promised great entertainment.

Therefore I followed . . . .

Essays

THE MAGICAL ASPECT OF THE LYRIC

One wonders, when attempting to drink the modern vintages of poetry, what sad and painful miracle has occurred that could change that which was so sweet, so fragrant and so rare to the palate of the soul into a bitter, tasteless and often unwholesome fluid. If we are lovers of that divine liquor brewed by the lordly minds of the past, recollection dawns within us, and abruptly we leave these coarsely-flavoured potions, thankfully returning to the never-ending draughts of wine pressed from the grapes of the past poets.

Here the spirit drinks from goblets abrim with fiery exultation; from vessels dark with the wine of lovely melancholy; from flasks of horn bubbling with the sparkling essences of love, life and laughter. A rich, splendid change has occurred, colour and thought evoked, that he drinks beverages distilled by mighty magicians.

Is it to be wondered at that the past students of this sublime art treated it with reverence and awe? For many, I believe, knew and understood the great powers of spiritual evocation that lay hidden within the often simple and gracious lines. They knew that the works of these masters were as temples in which the soul of their creator dwelt, and that he had climbed spiritual altitudes they had not yet traversed. But they also knew that by entering into these temples they would sense a little of that grandeur, unseen and unknown to the mass of mankind.

The above was written in regard to the lyric. I mean

[*Occult Review* (London), vol. 44, no. 7 (Jan. 1927): pp. 455–59.]

the true, regal lyric, burning with prophetic and emotional fervour, simple and crystalline in word and form; glittering with symbol and vision; and filled with the noble tones of divine melody. In this form of verse can be found philosophical concepts clarified and made beautiful for those minds that cannot grasp the tortuous methods indulged in by hazily minded thinkers. This is the form of verse that has given past civilisations ideals and strength to continue climbing upwards.

The poet of today revolts against these old conventional forms. He dethrones imaginative emotion and becomes the slave to a cold, soulless intellect that bristles with as many sharp points of criticism as does the porcupine with quills. He endeavours to concoct beverages from elements that refuse to mix. He produces synthetic substances that bear all the marks of artificiality, toil and artfulness, but certainly not of art. The sweat of his brow oozes from out every line, and the result makes painful reading. But the truth of the matter consists in this: He is not and will never be a poet until he realises that poetry is a spiritual power that will only serve those who are willing to become instruments of the Divine. And without this power, which is the vital spark of inspiration, he shapes but dead butterflies, dead flowers, dead birds. And though, like the alchemists of old, he may seek the informing principle that will give his creation perpetual life, he will constantly fail as long as barren intellect and scepticism are crowned king of his philosophy. Rhymed verse, unrhymed verse, shapely and unshapely, are utterly useless as long as his experimenting lacks this spiritual essence.

When one studies the great lyrics of the past, two principles are generally revealed, principles that endow the whole work with sincerity, beauty and power. And these are: a belief in God or gods, and in the ultimate nobility of the lowest of mankind.

"Agreed," one can imagine the modern poet saying, "but in those periods the pageantries of religion were in full bloom and faiths had not been destroyed by the explosives of Science. Today we know better, and can explain the workings of their minds by psychoanalytical methods. Their so-called divine imaginings were but transmuted sexual elements. Their sensitivity was but a form of neurasthenia. Their clairvoyance, particularly so in the case of William Blake, plain insanity that today would be certifiable." And he ceases, with probably a smile of contempt for the poets who believed, and for the present-day believers. And there he leaves us.

The true poet is a magician, particularly so in the case of the lyrical poet; for he has awakened certain centres that have enabled him to get in touch with the mind and elemental forces of Nature. We have only to read the works of Shelley to see the truth of this. And though it may be urged that Shelley was supposed to have been an atheist, his very work contradicts his belief. He was one in whom the sylph-nature predominated, to the exclusion of all else. The breeze, the cloud, the tempest and shower were enthralled into the verse of this enchanter of aerial powers. Subtle and elusive emotions were caught in the net of his inspiration, and transfixed, still lambent with life and fluttering their wings, upon paper. His voice is swift and light, and the frail cold flame that rushes through his lines sweeps the reader onwards. The dancing oreads were his playmates, Aurora his mother, and Aeolus his father. With Shelley we find one who was a natural pagan, and in perfect accord with the unresting spirit of Nature.

He, like all great and natural poets, was but an instrument, a tongue that translated the language of the elemental powers into the language of the nation. But these elemental powers sent forth a peculiar force possessing a mantric quality, and it was the mantra that immortalised the lyric, and likewise moulded its form. For the true poet does not have to measure and mould the vessel for the wine, as so many critics assume; but he becomes, in the truly mystical sense, one with his subject, and the form comes naturally.

Another aspect of mantric or lyrical poetry lies in the silence produced in the final line. If a lyric possesses the power to produce a cessation of mental turmoil, it has fulfilled its purpose. And here is another aspect that makes the poem great, though it could likewise be dangerous. For if this knowledge were used by one who desired to awaken the evil side in man, and had the genius to do so, he could create an unpleasant force in society, because the symbols, thoughts, colours and melodies enter the mind of the reader when the mind is stilled. The reader or listener becoming impersonal, does not oppose the forces invoked and flowing from the poem, and in that sacred silence a spiritual door is opened through which flows that spiritual power the poet felt when in the act of creation. In fact, the lover of poetry is subjected to a magical process, which is the reason for the suggestion that it would be dangerous to read the form of poetry that is loaded with unwholesome symbol, thought, and degenerating melody. Now, when speaking of the mantric quality in poetry, there is a further point to be considered, and that is the similarity of the forces invoked in verse. As an example, we will take three well-known poems, and it will be noted that a similar force flows from each. There is no need to quote them, for all who read verse know of them. They are: "Invictus" (William Ernest Henley), "Recessional" (Rudyard Kipling), and "Crossing the Bar" (Alfred Lord Tennyson). Although the authors of these three poems differ in genius to a considerable degree, yet, at the moment of composition, they had all attained a similar height of inspiration, and one of the loftiest and noblest peaks to which a poet could rise. For here the force invoked is compelling and masterful. And whereas other lyrics are scented, delicate and subtle, these verses are simple, direct, short, and pregnant with the dynamic quality of the spirit. In these three poems come aspiration, humility, and hope. Ambition, shaken and weakened, renews itself in the magic of "Invictus." Pride and majesty remember past failures at the altar of "Recessional." The soul becomes triumphant before the nobility of "Crossing the Bar." That is why it is suggested that they come from the highest altitudes, for the poets were then nearer to the source of things than probably at any other period of their lives. These are the trumpet tones that bring to us likewise a realisation of the existence of our Higher Selves. Poetry, from that aspect alone, becomes not merely the decorative embroidery of society, but a spiritual necessity, and will be recognised as such when the religious elements in man reawaken and establish their lost sovereignty in Nature.

Mention was previously made of psychoanalysis, a theory dealing with the anatomy, knots, and warps of the mind; a scientific maze, half-built, and becoming increasingly complicated by its exponents and opponents. As long as either side refuses to recognise the spiritual element, their complicated apparatus will solve only few of the problems.

Psychoanalysis is here alluded to in order to describe what it is believed takes place when the poet, or, for that matter, any artist becomes inspired.

The present-day belief is that inspiration, far from being a God-sent, holy flame, is the reverse; that it is a foul gas or fume rising from emotional and mental marshes which, by a strange moral process, becomes transmuted into some noble creation, some golden perfume, some idealistic concept, like the lotus rising from the mire. It is obvious that this ugliness can only be transformed by the caress and power of something finer and sweeter, but this can only be done when the soul makes a conscious effort to rise. Not that this emotion is necessarily changed into a spiritual force that creates beauty, but that, quite conceivably, it becomes a ladder or lever that the artist uses in order to lift himself up. For it is certainly a powerful force, which, in the process of coming in contact with the higher spheres, becomes likewise cleansed. Now when the poet achieves this summit, he is in a realm of new currents that are, as I have been told by an adept, of an emotional-mental nature; and if he is clairvoyant, he sees besides feeling the symbols that are within these spheres. Likewise he shows in his work an entirely new creative element. There are two reasons for this. One: He has become part of his Higher Self, and the Higher Self has a perfect individuality of its own, expressing itself in a new and original manner. Two: The sphere he has contacted has likewise peculiar properties of its own, and though, as mentioned above, some poets have entered similar spheres, it was the Higher Self that produced the differences so noticeable.

This is why poets become prophetic when speaking from these heights, and the proof that they have done so; for they have left the world of Time and can see that which is to come.

Let me conclude by quoting some of the instruction given me by the teacher to whom I have already alluded.

As occult students are aware, when the body sleeps the soul visits those realms that are of greatest interest to it. These realms are not astral but mental and spiritual.

In the higher planes, the artist has built up his own material, and many times assistance is given him in order that he may contact his own creative energy which he has established on the inner planes. Many poems are but poor translations of the poet's real inner themes, and often when out of the body one finds a poet studying his own poems and endeavouring to bring them down into a more material form so that he may remember them when in the Earth-consciousness.

Sometimes the poet reads his own works on the higher planes, then descends with it to a middle plane, striving to make this poem correspond with the knowledge of the middle plane; and here as well as on the higher plane he receives the aid of a teacher who attempts to impress the artist's mind with his material when he awakens on the physical plane. It is always the aim of these teachers who assist the artist to bring into incarnation a work of the nature of the higher spheres. Also, they endeavour to help the artist to keep that same vitality of thought-emotions that the work possesses on the inner realms. (M., quoted in Juste, *White Brother*, pp. 157–58)

The above quotation should serve as an illustration of the manner in which a poet produces his work, and why it possess the mantric quality.

Therefore, he who would be a poet must transmute the grey vibrations of this atmosphere into golden ones, and in the process he will discover that he has been treading a Path whose length terminates only at the porchway that opens upon the world of Divine Mysteries and secret chambers of Nature and of Godhood.

THE POWER OF THE PROPHET

I write of the prophet; or, as one can consider him to be, the divine eagle whose natural home is the golden eyrie of Paradise. He it is who has developed a spiritual militancy and strength, a nobility and graciousness, and a mind glowing with the deep fires of wisdom. For he has flown above the time-bound generations and, with compassion in his heart, pleaded for jewels from the gods to scatter and illuminate the souls and minds of mankind. He it is who bringeth morning and sweet waters for the imprisoned spirit; he it is who echoes the divine thunders of God, yet disturbs not the hare or the light petal of a flower, though his voice shaketh and crumbleth the fiery hate of Lucifer and his angels; he it is who singeth the hymns of the gods and translates their dreams for the keen-eared listeners of the world; and he it is was who helped to unfurl the blossoms of light throughout the past civilisations, and will do so throughout those that are to come. For the prophet is one who has been dipped and baptised in the flaming font of Heaven.

The prophet is a spiritual necessity: for he is the clear eyes in the brown of a blind humanity. A tree that stands erect in a crooked forest. For he is one who weighs and measures, with the impersonal power of intuition, the weaknesses and follies of the period in which he dwells. Through him the spirit of the future plants its seed, quickens within him, and is replanted in the spiritual soil of those who believe in him.

Though there have been many who have had a glimpse

[*Occult Review* (London), vol. 45, no. 3 (Mar. 1927): pp. 178–82.]

of the future, I write of those who, I believe, had a truer consciousness and understanding of this power of prophecy; and they are the inspired messengers and founders of new religions. And it is because of their importance to the development of humanity that I write this article. Today they are considered the psychological throwback of the social body. Scientists hold that the prophet was but the clever visionary or lawgiver to an ignorant people; a high-caste witch-doctor to an emotional and unanalytical nation. And I believe whoever is blind to the things of the spirit will deem him to be so. For the spirit of a man learns truths by the use of symbols, and they who deny the existence of the spirit do not know the alphabet of the spirit, and so being illiterate cannot read the truths symbolised by the prophet.

Above the physical, emotional, and mental turmoil of humanity he stands, beyond the three dark atmospheres that confuse and bind the soul of man to Time; and there set free from the distorting elements, he prepares the roads of light for those whose hearts are parched, whose eyes are dimmed and whose minds are darkened. And from his rare, clean altitude his ears are keener to the voices of the future, and his eyes watch the mighty arms of the gods wheel this globe to the scenes their companions have brooded upon and created for the unsuspecting souls of Earth.

Now the clay of the prophet is of a rare sensitive substance, for the higher altitude in which he moves when inspired purifies and sweeps away any evil that may cling to him; and that is one of the reasons why we read of the prophet ascending the mountains; and in the higher realms this is literally true, for evil cannot rise to great heights. And it is on these higher altitudes that they commune with those who dwell nearer to the source of divine realities, bringing back with them wisdom and thoughts made luminous and overbrimming with beauty. These thoughts are given to him to withhold or scatter as he may think fit. For within the prophet dwells much understanding, and any message that he gives is given with a thorough knowledge as to the psychological limitations of that nation or group into which he has incarnated.

But their messages are not for the physical body alone, but for the imprisoned soul which seeks freedom and desire to express itself. And in this manner the message of the prophet stirs the mind to respond to the Higher Self within; and, though generation after generation deadens the voice and blurs the visions of the prophet, yet, ultimately, the body will be compelled to attend and obey the message that the soul has heard, even though they were heard in other incarnations.

Now the age in which we live has become prolific in prophecy and loud with the sounds of their voices. They predict calamities, the dawning of a new age, and the coming of a Messiah. Threats, warnings, prayers, issue from their lips in an ever-increasing flood. And the result is that they who listen are bewildered. And rightly so. The skein of incidents to come are so entangling, so broken up that it seems impossible to weave all into a harmonious pattern. And from it all comes the question: "Whom are we to believe?" Now one thing is obvious: the prophet must have developed powers that should give him clear sight, and, as I mentioned elsewhere, he must speak from a higher plane. In short, he must develop a higher mental and spiritual clairvoyance. And if he can do so, it is a sign of the true adept; for, according to the teachings given me, the white adept, or magician, cannot enter the higher planes unless he is pure and has achieved a certain soul-development. This means that the higher elementals would oppose his attempts to enter if he had not attained. And now, having striven to give what I hope is a clear conception as to what powers a prophet should possess, I shall now quote from some of the information given to me by my teacher:

A student who has been able to pass through the severe regimes demanded by his teacher is shown those sources from whence information may be derived. There are schools in which, if he is eligible, he may pursue such studies as seership and prophecy. There are different institutions on these higher planes that deal with prophecy in its different aspects. In one college, one can read the chronicle of the past, present and future, as Time is measured on this sphere. In another college named the College of the Seers, one can learn to visualise from a high altitude of consciousness the events which are taking place on Earth; and by correlating his experiences in vision with the incidents on Earth, he can determine, to a large degree, the natural course of events.

There is a College of Chronicles, wherein records and plans of the past and future are stored; the College of the Seers and the School of the Prophets. These colleges are visited and instruction given. Here the student is tested and trained to observe and understand the events which are to take place in the lower spheres.

The question I asked my teacher was in regard to

the method whereby one could know the true prophet from the false. And here is the answer:

The prophet is an instrument through which flows the impersonal force known as Truth. And few can stand the presentment of truth. And the prophet has been given truth in the form of *mental attributes*. This form of attribute is a consciousness rendered forth from Justice. If Justice is also Truth, then this attribute is that illuminative quality that awakens the nodes of consciousness within a man's mind, these nodes being in the likeness of the consciousness of Justice.

The above can be explained in this manner: The mental body of man possesses certain centres of consciousness that lie dormant until a certain truth similar to that centre strikes it. The result is that the centre responds and recognises the truth. Then comes the awakening, that awakening that to the person involved may be a form of illumination, or recollection and realisation of a belief the person would never have accepted previously.

Now the prophet knows of these centres, being, as I have said before, an adept as well as a mystic; and in his studies he is taught to understand the minds to whom he is speaking. That, I think, explains why each great religion has had a different form of ceremony and exercise. For these rites and ceremonies were not created in order to hypnotise disciples into belief but in order that they might develop certain attributes possessed only by them. There are many different forms of consciousness, and the prophet taps that form of consciousness that is flowing towards this planet for a certain group. Each group has its leader, and for them his message is understood. Thus there are many kinds of prophets, and many of these prophets can only appeal and evoke a response from the group to which he belongs. And that is the reason why his appeal to other minds may fall upon stony ground.

Further teachings are:

There are many divisions of prophecy, for it has much to do with the law of Justice, and the prophet must be careful, *for to assume the attitude of a prophet is also to assume the responsibility which such a prophet's utterance may bring him.* The art of the prophet is the generalisation of events and the summing up of their manifestations in their entirety. The prophet must also realise how much the law allows him to render forth and he must work according to the Law which governs the giving forth of true prophecy. In other words, the student must be very careful in the giving forth of knowledge which he has gained during his schooling in the higher spheres, and he must be prepared to assume the responsibility incurred to the clan or brotherhood of which he is a member, for, as most students do not realise, a student initiated into a brotherhood becomes at-one-ment with the group, and any word issuing form his mouth is judged not only by his Higher Self, but by the members about him, and until he has been able to build within his own character and nature of his being that stability which is of the nature of Truth and Justice he is apt to be censured by the wardens of the College, who then determine how far he should be allowed to progress in the wisdom and knowledge of prophetic utterance.

The above teaching proves, I think, to those who believe in the existence of higher realms, that prophecy is another aspect of scientific occultism. It is not a mere blind inspiration or an intense emotionalism, though obviously emotion enters into it—for the language of the higher spheres is in picture-form, and certain thought-emotions that reach the prophet who translates these pictures and emotions into the language of the country—but a clear and scientific understanding, the result of a scientific training in spiritual things. But this should not blind us to the fact that the prophet is great, for he has achieved an initiation into spiritual heights that has made him indeed godlike.

There is another aspect of prophecy that may explain much that bewilders us, and that is in regard to the number of teachers who write upon spiritual and mystical things and who are continually prophesying. This, I understand, is the explanation: When a group of souls pass over they are still participants in the religion they left on earth. And these groups endeavour to find instruments for their message. I have been told that many of the prophets of today are these instruments, who are greatly influenced by the mass-mind and consciousness of these groups who are working upon another plane; and they give to their instruments teachings and inspiration that, to the medium, appears to come direct from God. Now this has two sides: Much of the knowledge may be false and much may be true. And that can only be proved by the student finding out whether they possess a sense of responsibility or otherwise. If otherwise, watch them with great care. I think the above aspect also explains why a number of prophets may give forth a similar teaching though they may dwell in different lands and be far apart, for the similarity may be caused by the fact that the consciousness of these teachers is of the same spiritual order; although I admit that one could say that the prophecies are the same because truth is a thing that cannot be argued about. But I think the proof of a person being illuminated consists in the fact as to whether he has a sense of responsibility or otherwise, as I mentioned elsewhere. Now, if he is truly illuminated, one of the first things he will know—and this cannot be emphasised too strongly—is that he cannot command, for he knows that man is a servant to one higher than he: one who knows whither and why the soul moves onward, and the time and place when knowledge should be given—and that power is the soul's Higher Self. And it is for this reason that the true prophet does not enforce or expect obedience. He only guides and suggests.

Only by making man conscious of the existence of a Higher Self within him does the prophet help humanity, for in that manner he builds a bridge from this planet to the infinite dominions of the spirit; and it will be in that manner that the laws of God and Justice will come to pass and ultimately reign over Earth.

THE THREE LAWS OF FREEDOM

Ever since the mind of man flamed into consciousness, there has been, at some period of his life, a certain altitude he has attempted to climb; a height looming clearly in the days of persecution, and attained to in the days of happiness; a height surrounded by an atmosphere of perpetual spring, lit by the light of the sun, and made clean by the pure winds of the spirit. From this summit man sees more clearly the path of his development and finds the sieve that sifts the rare grains of Truth from the common grains of Error. It is towards this summit that souls must travel ere they can begin their conscious pilgrimage towards Godhead. And Freedom is its name.

There is only one caste in humanity possessing the true understanding of freedom, and this is composed of those who have achieved a certain illumination in the spiritual sense. One can call them mystic-occultists, an unfettered group of wise students who understand the clear, yet hidden, laws created by God. They are free because they are wise enough not to trample down the freedom of others. The rest are not free, never have been free; though all possess a certain amount of free-will. Democratic nations and autocratic nations are both bound by the same fetters. To the spiritual eye, the wealthy man is clothed in the same tattered rags as the beggar; for all are thinly clothed who do not wear the royal raiment of freedom. To the spirit, that is the only costume that matters; for, according to the teachings given me, the soul desires three things: Freedom, Love, Creation. Freedom is the prerogative of all souls,

[*Occult Review* (London), vol. 47, no. 3 (Mar. 1928): pp. 165–69.]

though few realise it; and they who would limit the freedom of man, limit, I understand, their own freedom when they pass over: living in a half-comatose state, desiring freedom, but unable to break the shell they had created. In some cases I have seen these people who have imprisoned themselves on account of their lack of tolerance. Some have been so imprisoned for centuries. I have seen them dressed in the costumes of the period in which they lived. But it may interest the student to know that many also attempt to return the evil they did by doing good, and thus repair the damage.

In the mind of the adolescent this desire for freedom is very strong, and revolt against old customs and laws signifies its appearance. After adolescence it usually disappears, but within the hearts of a few it lingers, and they generally become the forerunners of the too-slowly moving caravan of humanity. Usually, such are in closer and happier relationship with the spirit within them, seeking to obey its commands, and so possessing a broader outlook upon life; for the closer we are in communion with our Higher Selves, so much more freewill do we possess.

I believe our ideals and dreams of sweeter things are the invocations of our Higher Selves desiring this liberty, thus producing that restlessness within man that makes him a pioneer, a creator of the arts, a builder of new civilisations; but also, if such a creative season comes to the soul of man, it comes only because that soul has planted in its wintry past the seeds necessary for such a time.

Now when speaking of freedom we do not mean independence as understood by the majority; that form of freedom is but the ego suffering from a form of mental elephantiasis. The freedom we mean is the realisation that all should be permitted to express themselves and work in harmony with the laws of Nature.

Therefore it is that the truly spiritual are free. They see with inner vision the heavy and terrible chains of the past that imprison the individual and the nation, chains created through ignorance and arrogance. My teacher once described to me how he saw with inner vision the result of a selfless deed by a friend. Immediately this friend made the sacrifice, a great chain dropped form her.

Now this desire for freedom has, within recent years, brought many strange children to birth. The clumsy body and illogical mind of Democracy has been reared, holding in her arms the loudly bawling, crimson-faced infant namcd Socialism; and many another queer child has followed in its wake. For a great ideal is like a mental emperor, ruling the minds of many who serve and gladly obey its commands. A man in whom such an ideal incarnates has behind him a stupendous power. It is he who pours this spiritual tonic into those willing to drink, renewing them with strength and releasing them from old conditions. All this proves how deeply implanted is this desire for freedom. The democratic spirit, so strong today, is, we believe, the Higher Self of a nation striving to express itself, but doing so imperfectly because of the imperfections of the instrument. For this Higher Self brings with it a mental force that stirs the minds of its human atoms, illuminating and broadening their vision of things.

Now in this age this force is rapidly being freed, not by the conquerors—conquerors are rarely generous —but by the conquered; and deaf and sightless is that man and that nation who cannot hear and see these portents. The gods are unlocking the dungeons wherein Freedom has long lain manacled, and the clang of her falling fetters brings new courage into the hearts of the enslaved, and an uneasiness into the hearts of their oppressors.

There is a certain feeling abroad, felt by many sensitive and clairvoyant people, that we are entering into a new era, an era of justice wherein freedom in all its aspects will be expressed. This, we understand, is an influence that comes at certain turnings in the journeyings of our planet, a cyclic and pre-ordained development, rather than the repair of some divine and age-old accident, as many believe.

If the minds of the past were imprisoned by narrow and dogmatic beliefs of religion and philosophy, they were but necessary experiences for the soul, forcing it to realise the value and importance of freedom, for the Higher Self can express Itself only when It is free. I think that the finest expression of freedom is to be found in children, because they are nearer to the Spirit and are therefore protected.

Now when thinking of freedom, there is an aspect man has seldom considered: that aspect being freedom in relationship to Nature. Man has usually considered Nature to be an unconscious power, unaware of our actions, unaware of our methods of using her. If man only realised, however, that Nature also has a mind and wish for self-expression, he would work in much greater harmony and produce results as great, if not greater, than those produced by past civilisations. Today we think of Nature not as an entity, but as a number of unconscious forces, working, in some miraculous manner, in a perfectly harmonious fashion; a belief manifestly absurd when examined fearlessly and impersonally. Nature is only dead and unresponsive to those who are dead and unresponsive to her. There is a mind in Nature that feels the thwartings of man as keenly as the personality; and it is this thwarting of her freedom that forces Nature to rebel. And the elements all respond. We have had earthquakes, tornadoes, volcanoes, all in great activity within the past few years, and what to us is abnormality in Nature's movements is really a return of Nature to her normal state. Nature is not a willing servant to an ignorant and unclean master, a master who in the past has interfered with her methods, denuding lands of trees and plaguing them with alien forms of life, ignorantly placed there by man.

If we glance round and question the calamities constantly taking place, and the unrest in the hearts of men, we will recognise that some hidden energy is at work besides that released from the oppression of nations and the pressure of changing environments. This energy is changing, slowly but surely, the minds of those responding to its influence. It is, I believe, the power of the awakening gods, who are the agents of the majestic consciousness of Nature, a consciousness that is slowly being freed as man repays his debt to the past and makes himself fit to enter into the new age.

Here, then, are three aspects of the one principle that must be realised ere man can resolve the disharmony in which he lives: freedom for the soul of each being; freedom for each nation; and finally, and most difficult of all, an understanding and recognition of Nature's consciousness, and an endeavour to work in harmony with her forces.

By way of conclusion a few teachings bearing on the subject given me by my teacher may fittingly round off this article:

In many places are those who can teach the student

to enter into harmonious relationship with the great Demeter; but there is a great struggle before the student ere she unveils her face. There are specially trained beings, partly human, partly elemental, who test the aspirant, lending him filaments of their more subtle and purer bodies to help him bridge that gap between his higher and lower self which separates him from *his kingdom in Nature*. Man was born to be a sovereign ruler in these interior worlds, but he will not be allowed entry if he fails to apprehend and obey their laws.

We have not built up an instrument sensitive enough to record Nature's finer vibrations; and to do so is the ABC of occultism. How can we enter her consciousness? How can we commune with her unless we build within ourselves those diaphragms which respond to her finer elements? We must remember that though Nature is an all-embracing mother; she will not call to us if we are to be destructive forces in her kingdoms. Her wisdom is not our wisdom, and she is strong and imperative in demand and will not allow us to disturb her serenity.

This is why, at times, the student becomes a hermit. He often fails for the first and second time to enter into the consciousness of Nature. But sometimes he is successful, for there are many ministering beings to the soul; and at the time, when faint-hearted and discouraged, he is about to return to the normal life of man, he suddenly finds there will come to him that for which he has been seeking so long. For he had renounced all desire for this attainment, believing it impossible, or that it was not for him. And true renunciation often brings to man God's realisation. All have to follow this path. Do not be discouraged, for the great mother watches over her indolent children and smiles on their smallest efforts to regain union with her presence. But how hard a struggle it is to become an instrument for Nature's purpose. Your greatest help is that inner self within the garment you have moulded and modelled for its use. Freedom is the power to be; to become an instrument to work in harmony and to realise the Law which is behind all things.

All the above implies that if man endeavoured to approach Nature with understanding and sympathy he would get to know of her reality and would unlock, through sympathetic response, the elemental powers. Then would follow stupendous changes in the features of this planet. Old religions would return; temples would be built; and man would revert, not to a sensual and picturesquely evil form of paganism, but to a clean and holy paganism, wherein the gods would commune and help mankind in his attempt to gain wisdom and knowledge of their powers. Then, when the over-patched costumes that cloaked the simple creeds of the past have been flung aside, the clear laughter of Arcadia will ring over a golden world, and Truth and Freedom will be the acknowledged sovereigns of humanity.

THOUGHTS ON THE "TWO PATHS"

It appears, when studying the above subject, that the mind of man is incapable of making a synthesis of his theories. Either he is a mystic or an occultist; just as one is either a Christian or a Buddhist; a Conservative or a Socialist. Men are always particles of things; never a whole, never a unity. Such unsatisfactory methods of thought lead to the unsolved problems: "What path should man travel in order to attain perfection? Is the path of mysticism better than the occult path? Is the path of occultism better than the mystic path?" That the true path is a combination of both seldom enters the mind of the student. To use one method only is as absurd as would be the action of a person using only one sense out of five and disdaining the use of the rest. If we met such a person we would look upon him in amazement. Yet this is what a great number of students persist in doing: dividing that which needs no division.

Man, we are told, is made in the likeness of God. If that is so, and God, who is love, is also wisdom, then, obviously, man who is potentially a god should likewise attempt to develop all his attributes. Just as primitive man evolved from a simple state of society to a more complex, so should the mystic eventually evolve from the stone age of divinity to a fuller and more complex state of divinity.

In the past hermits atrophied many attributes and desires in order to attain to spiritual revelation—an unwise action, for it prevented the expression of the complete revelation owing to the destruction of the

[*Occult Review* (London), vol. 48, no. 3 (Sept. 1928): pp. 182–85.]

instruments through which much of this illumination came. Today many mystics do likewise, atrophying the intellectual instrument to the detriment of complete divine realisation. The occultist acts otherwise. In his view, every particle of the body has its purpose; and perfect health is one of the most important qualifications for students of this subject. For the occultist knows he is surrounded by numerous hidden forces that all have their part to play in the development of man to mastership. The necessity for a perfectly healthy and virile body cannot be emphasised too strongly.

The emotions of the mystic are often aflame, and he sometimes develops beautiful pinions; but usually he does not know where to fly. And the winds of other planes blow him here and there, and he has to follow their courses. He may find his wings in the gold of the sun, the silver of the moon, or the blue of the sky; and his soul may sparkle with the fair enamels of all the virtues; yet, if his mind is undeveloped, all these qualities are as useless as he in whom the heart qualities are undeveloped. For he is but a decorative symbol of Heaven and little else. What is necessary is an illumination for the mental principles as well as for the emotional. Man being blind in the mass, why should the more highly developed types persist in maintaining merely a higher form of blindness?

The teacher of mysticism often gives to his disciples the soft pillows of faith; and upon these the weary-hearted are told to rest and await the moment when God will fill them with an inner radiance. But though clouded illumination may create a temporary happiness, happiness is not wisdom. The mystic may saturate his emotions in the perfumes of love; but neither is that wisdom. Wisdom is the highest of all things, because it is the purest distillation of knowledge and love.

The true occultist is taught differently from the mystic. He is told to take an active part in his endeavours to acquire wisdom; he is told to observe and understand how to weave the raiment of the spirit with his own hands, and not wait for some outside power to weave and robe him in it. He is taught where to find the threads for this holy garment; and how to design the pattern best fitted for his character. And because of his experiences he also knows how to discern the false teacher from the true. For by faith alone—not that faith is other than necessary in the pursuit of occult knowledge—the mystic may never eat of the sweet fruits of divinity.

The occultist desires to peer into the world's crystal and read therein the secrets of existence and of man's pilgrimage. He wishes to know how the fabric of illusion has been woven, upon what hidden loom the laws of Nature have been spun.

Occultism is the science of the spirit; mysticism is the emotion of the spirit. Occultism can make man godlike; mysticism can make man angelic. The mystic is one who has incarnated, but often refuses to accept the fact. The occultist accepts the fact, but also attempts to discover his place in the work of the world. The mystic attempts to prune the wilderness of the world with blunted shears; the occultist before any such attempt sharpens them upon the keen grindstone of the intellect. The ecstasies of the mystic burn intermittently, because he seldom gets in permanent touch with those spiritual principles that will add fuel to his aspirations. It is true he may get a sudden and golden glimpse of the majesty of God; but how much wiser he would be if he could manage to be permanently conscious of such a vision? Thus, though the mystic may bring into existence a gem, it is usually an uncut gem. Rare it may be, but its beauty and radiance do not shine out as clearly as when it is ground and made symmetrical by the polishing tool of intelligence. Though ecstasy tells the mystic God exists, that does not give him the power of discrimination. Today, man is developing an analytical power of perception; and this necessary attribute must not be ignored. What is necessary today is to help humanity break through the many illusions surrounding his mental body; not to concentrate on the emotional body. When speaking of the mind, however, the occultist does not mean the lower mind, which is surrounded by illusions, but the Higher Mind, wherein one can obtain clear vision and understanding.

"Yet," one will ask, "what exactly are the qualities needed in occultism?" First, and most important, is the necessity for balance. The occult student must be vital on all planes, possessing just as great an emotional capacity as the mystic, but knowing when and where to use it. He must not give way to sentiment, as the mystic often does. The occultist must have a scientific outlook on things. He must persevere in his practices, and be strong in will. In short, he must use every particle in his nature; for by constantly exercising them he becomes flexible yet resistant to all around him. For surely it is no compliment to the Creator of man that the soul should become like a limp piece of rag?

When speaking of the occultist, one does not mean the scholastic researcher into occultism—one who makes painstaking researches in often unimportant directions—but the genuine student who is under the tutelage of one who knows his subject, and who can demonstrate what he has to teach. Possibly the reason why occultism is so often shunned is because it usually brings to mind the evil practices of black magic. It is true that occultism can show such a side, and man today usually thinks of the evil aspect; but that can only be when the love-principles are not well developed. Therefore it is essential, as I have said before, that the occultist should develop all attributes of character.

Often the mystic is permitted to gaze into the palace of the spirit; but soon afterwards he falls back into the hovel of the clay, a sad-hearted, sighing man, praying ceaselessly for a glimpse once again into this splendid dwelling. The light of it had dazzled his eyes, and the glory of it had given him temporary happiness; but not knowing how to keep his foothold in such a place, he is unhappy, dissatisfied with the meannesses of the world, yet rarely able to enter into his spiritual inheritance. Only with a rounded character; wise in the knowledge of God; strong in will; filled with a balanced love and understanding for all things can he stand above the chaos of this world.

SUBTERRANEAN PAGANISM

It is interesting to note the steady and subtle return to pagan ideas and ideals. The ancient Gods are creeping back through many hidden doors of human thought; some through the more extreme development of Psychoanalysis; others via the philosophies of ancient Greece; some through an interest in psychical research and the discovery of elemental forces; some through the practice of magic and its rituals and some even through an investigation into telepathy and radiation, and strange solutions are revealed; for the unorthodox approach of today was the orthodox approach of two thousand years ago and this discloses the inter-relationship forbidden by certain religious vested interests.

This study and technique of the Mysteries gives such colour to the emotions and such revelations to the mind that, once liberated from the cell of an intolerant creed, they never return.

The religions of today are then seen in their true perspective; devitalised because the gates have been closed against the Gods, and spiritually illiterate because their minds have been closed against the intuitions.

[*Catalogue and Review* (London: Atlantis Bookshop, 1947), p. 9.]

HARVESTER

A walk with a wise man can be filled with the unusual;
for his mind is outstretched, a subtle net aware and alert
for the floating idea; the apparent trivial that might hide
treasure. He is not at the mercy of his subconscious
—that chamber of tattered fragments and stale mem-
oires; to the wise man the atmosphere nourishes him
with fresh vital force.

Sometimes the air is rich with radiance he only sees;
the banners from unseen battlements float in the shining
heavens—the insignia of incorruptible realms. Some-
times a line—burnished and complete—a perfected
trinket—comes suddenly upon him.

There are no set seasons for his harvestings; these
come to him without warning; new views, new flashes
of illumination. Those who have the gift of vision always
have abundance; but to the spiritually colourless, this
is a colourless land.

[*Catalogue and Review* (London: Atlantis Bookshop, 1947), pp. 13–14.]

THE MASTER CONSCIOUSNESS

They have evolved their animal consciousness into a condition of purified light and as this consciousness ascends into the brighter lands ever-greater control is established over the lower mind. This is the divine destiny of each being.

[*Catalogue and Review* (London: Atlantis Bookshop, 1947), p. 15.]

APHORISMS

In youth I saw man as a fallen angel; when I grew older
I saw him as an ape; now I see him as an evolving animal.

There has rarely been a teacher's pupil who has not
lessened the quality of the teachings.

A platitude is stale wisdom.

Proverbs are the lazy man's leaning posts.

A star to a mystic is the handiwork of God; to the sci-
entist, a cosmic mechanism; but to the philosopher a
star may be a hundred things, reveal a thousand mean-
ings—probably all wrong.

Spiritual evolution is an ever greater capacity for dis-
criminating choice.

Wisdom appeals to the intuition; reason, to the intel-
lect; and oratory, to the emotions; but in a parable the
master interweaves all three.

Ritual is symbolic pattern in active manifestation.

[*Catalogue and Review* (London: Atlantis Bookshop, 1947), p. 15.]

THE ART OF WISDOM

Nature does not sidestep growth; neither can the student. An immature mind cannot teach wisely; how can a mind that has made only half the journey and has therefore seen only half the way tell what the rest of the road is like? True wisdom, which is the result of maturity, possesses an art all its own. To the simple mind the answer to a problem is given in the form of a parable; to the intellectual mind the reply should be scientific, logical and clear; to the mystic it can be given as a standard of conduct.

The mind of a wise man is radiant with light when the qualities of human character are kept under control, and such minds are all embracing comprehension and compassion. This rich, mellow consciousness deals with truth as an artist treats colour on a canvas. He knows the true age of the inquirer and knows the age-old truths must be given a new pattern and tint so that the inquirer will go away feeling he has been presented with something precious and unique. And this is a very great art—perhaps the greatest—for the traveller is given a touch of illumination to his consciousness; an immortal fragment that will add to his final liberation. This is the art of the spirit, as a composition is art to a composer. Spiritual truths are given to men in many forms, but wisdom is an essence that is more subtle and deeper than all.

The wise man takes the colours of the spiritual truths, the brushes of material substance, and uses human

[*Catalogue and Review* (London: Atlantis Bookshop, 1947), pp. 20–21. Reprinted and signed "QUAESTOR" in *Occult Observer* (London), vol. 1, no. 5 (1950): p. 332.]

consciousness as his canvas; and the perfect blend might be an immortal phrase, a shining parable, or a burning whiplash in a sentence; for wisdom must also be strong when necessary and also gay with laughter as the wise man knows that laughter besides strength and beauty is part of wisdom.

HOW IMPORTANT IS THE STUDY OF
OCCULTISM?

How useful are occult principles in our everyday activities? In the art of living? In the solution to vital problems: economic, psychologic, spiritual?

Are occult philosophies and systems the fantasies of escape? Can they give warmth and glow to those in spiritual coldness? Can they give cover to the mentally naked and provide protection for the emotionally hurt? For if this complicated subject is examined by the unbiased and critical intellect one discovers so much confusion and absurdity; so much taken for granted without demonstrability that contempt is frequently justified.

There is only ONE occult science; but there are thousands of ways to it. There are also numerous branches stemming from this science; but only one of each of these branches can be correct. The others are pseudo and uncertain and therefore undemonstrable.

Unfortunately there has grown—through the centuries—a thick crust of doctrine, fogs of tradition, the folklore of peasants and the entangling interpretations of philosophers. In this vast terrain of jungle and marsh and abyss appear self-constituted guides; many well-meaning, some who have had a few flashes of illumination, some who have read the wrong books and believe they are going the right way because they have sincere motives, and a few—a very few—to whom have been given hints of the true science.

Now light-heartedly, without clear perspective, without knowledge of longitudes and latitudes, they

[*Occult Observer* (London), vol. i, no. i (May 1949): pp. 2–4.]

scramble and wander about these nebulous worlds, and the spiritual quest sometimes becomes a farce, sometimes a tragedy; sometimes they break through these barriers and discover one of the hidden sciences.

Only then does occultism become important in the way of life and of wisdom. Then previous claimants are seen at their true value: all the correct or incorrect approaches had served some useful purpose, for they had taught discrimination; but now a hint of the vast and sublime edifice is revealed. They now find that though hidden it is dynamic and charged with the potent and secret interplay of influences and forces through the microcosm: the true esotericism, so smoothly used but never revealed.

Now true and false relationships are seen: here is not only revelation but revolution; meaning is given to what was meaningless; the hidden mechanics appear without the vapours of theories and speculation; both glib and gloomy interpretations are revealed in their true ignorance and narrowness and impertinence; and negative ways of life are contemptuously discarded: the joyless puritanism of the unbalanced.

Only the strong and the passionate can rend these various veils; only strong eyes face this spiritual blaze, and just as an engine pulsates with power so should they who would become gods; for the kingdoms of the true heavens are not for the emotional eunuchs, the arid and the colourless. Self-deception knits more veils of illusion than it ever unravels. Neither can any of the branches of these secret sciences be used if the human mechanisms are distorted, weak or incomplete.

Unfortunately many confuse flabbiness with goodness and believe that bright and clean outlines of character and strength can spring from the sapless nature of a negative morality; not appreciating that the batteries of the body must be powerfully charged, vibrant with many forms of strength in order to bring any occult science into practical everyday use.

Here emerges the usefulness and importance of occultism which takes numerous forms and many names; for these techniques are not called "occult." The great artist unconsciously applies projection and attunement to his work; the successful businessman uses, unknowingly, a form of clairvoyance; the inspired doctors, correct diagnosis; the poet, powers of prophecy. Beethoven, Mozart, Shakespeare and Milton heard the great pulsations of the higher realms and recorded them.

These are your true occultists: geniuses who have perfected vehicles through many incarnations, the masters; comprehensive in their visions and in their works yet who may never use the term *occult* but who make glorious practical use of their powers for the benefit of humanity. Whoever brings man more light and opens the way to individual liberation, reveals to us our own inner richness, and proves the importance of occultism in our everyday activities.

MAGIC AND ART

All the high moments in art are magical in quality; that is, have an untranslatable and indefinable influence that is unforgettable; for a vital consciousness enters in just as life enters an organism and makes it move. Critics endeavour to analyse it—and fail. Students try to imitate but unsuccessfully; and the envious belittle it, but are themselves forgotten.

Now a great work of art is also a spiritual mystery; for the artist has pierced many veils, probed beyond the illusions into the permanent, and a hint—fragrant with infinite richness and intensity—has been given. And this enduring loveliness, whether distilled into words or music, into colour or stone, is given to man. A great adventure has been recorded; a spiritual illumination has been saturated in virtue, which gathers—strangely enough—strength through the ages.

To analyse this elusive magic is impossible; as well try to analyse the divine; for even the artist cannot analyse this gift though he has captured and expressed it. Magic, like electricity, can be used, but not defined.

The great artist has no necessity to be consciously revolutionary as his inspirations are of a unique nature and comprehensive sense. Neither does he express his age; he expresses himself through the medium of his age, which is vastly different. The great artist, though frequently prophetic, can be equally retrospective and can incorporate in his work as much of the past as he does the future. His mind ranges over far greater perspectives in visions and in ideas, and it is not because he

[*Occult Observer* (London), vol. 1, no. 1 (May 1949): p. 57.]

is ahead of his time that makes him either prophetic or retrospective, but because he is above his time; though this quality would be exceedingly rare, as such a quality would defeat one of the purposes of art: to be a bridge between lower and Higher man.

QUAESTOR

THE DIGNITY OF OCCULTISM

In the beginning there are the small darknesses: the mind in chaos, and for many there is no Genesis. They are born and they move and they die within a long night. Cradled in chaos, they drift indifferently on, without curiosity or purpose; and of such is the kingdom of the unawakened.

Now for a few, the waters of the mind are suddenly stirred: whether through vision or voice, there flashes the swift light of the soul; darkness is rent and the senses know they have been sleeping. But bright intimations reveal more than a purpose; they reveal that some-where are hidden El Doradoes, bright territories, the Hesperides, veiled and welcoming. Yet these secret terri-tories are neither forbidden nor imaginary; neither have the mysteries been lost nor forgotten; but the way to these places must be earned, and inflated values about oneself will not be recognised.

When the mind reaches more profound levels, it dis-covers a richness as though thought had been dipped into reservoirs of royal dye—tyrian purples of the im-agination—activities and relationships to godlike forms and celestial matters; and these flash hints and volts of wisdom; fragments from a cosmic unity; messages from secret citadels.

Occultism is essentially aristocratic; though its bound-aries are wider than this world, it demands from its true subjects integrity and straightness. Thus few discover or are permitted to find the secret door. Beyond all the mysteries reigns wisdom, whose qualities dignify, whose

[*Occult Observer* (London), vol. 1, no. 2 (Summer 1949): pp. 65–70.]

understanding raises up those who would follow from the dust and decay of this world.

Glib solutions by scientists only solve material discomforts, but completely fail in the subtler fields of phenomena. Crude reasoning has led to a monstrous and paralysing dark; though with the use of reason and mechanics, faith and muddled theologies could no longer be acceptable; for the traditional religions had long ago cast aside the spiritual mechanics called under other names: magic, alchemy, divination and astral forces —with the taunt of "paganism and idolatry"; but left a gulf, a place without foundations; a state of emptiness to be filled in by theological fantasy and scientific speculation; though neither intelligible to the intuition nor to the reason; for both emphasised in the narrowest of limits—human dogma.

It is an unhappy fact that the sciences either ignored or treated with contempt the occult techniques. Yet in the earliest literature of mankind, hints of man's relationship with the gods have been revealed, systems described and conveyed through the written word and through the rituals of secret societies.

The orthodoxies having failed you and turned you upon yourself; you must turn spiritual navvy and dig; yet into no soft clay but into a subtle and slippery one. And it is, as far as you can ascertain, a perilous task. Like labouring in a cave with only an occasional flicker of the intuition to guide. You are also doubtful concerning the existence of any treasure. If only the words "Open Sesame" could be used; and behold! all the glitter and opulence of cosmic treasure be revealed.

Only when reaching responsibility are the psychological and spiritual structures of the Universe permitted to be comprehended; before that, they seem unsolvable mysteries. The intellectual stares through the mist of his arrogance and there is darkness; the mystic sees through vortices of emotion and senses an amorphous unity.

If there is a secret and hidden architecture, a complicated pattern and plan operating and overshadowing our lives, why is mankind left in ignorance of such forces? Because such systems are beyond eye-range must they be non-existent? Many leaders, being equally blind and impressed by scientific data, add to the bewilderment of the inquirer. Yet such blindness and crudity applies only to a small section of humanity: the West. The superstitious, ignorant East knows better; their fears and superstitions, their rituals and taboos have evolved from records of an ancient arcanum, astral-life memories during sleep, and sensitivity to elemental entities who are always with them. From the primitive sensitive emerges a wholesome respect for the unknown with childish interpretations of the Universe; but from the spiritualised sensitive, aware of similar phenomena, comes a love and adoration and great wisdom-teaching: for both accept the activity and existence of these hidden territories and peoples.

"But why are we of the West without this knowledge?" This question is constantly asked. One could give many reasons. The scientific hoi poloi, the intellectual lumpen-proletariat, the dithering theologian and many philosophers whose gullets are choked with discussions and whose minds are a debris of prolegomena; all have succeeded in having the astral gates slammed upon them through conceit and self-interest; though admittedly they are unaware of being locked out. Groping within their own darkness, they denounce and deny:

patronising the sensitive and compelling the confused to accept their interpretations. Finding no place or crevice for their grubby minds to enter the protective walls of spiritual places, they declare them to be non-existent.

With peevish bias the materialist bludgeons and attacks dreamer and prophet, denying the nobler horizons they might see. Such are the mental generals and captains over the armies of man today; though beyond their small and tragic victories, over their helots, hidden yet dynamic are the galaxies of consciousness, the splendid forerunners, those who have ascended and who have refined—through countless incarnations—the shining defenders of the occult faith, who guard their treasures from the clamorous and conceited urchins of mankind.

The mysteries are aloof and keep their silent counsels. Their protections are subtle, and though the minds of the unready and inquisitive may probe and reach out, if they occasionally glance through the gates, they usually misinterpret the moment of vision and blink it out as a result of an ill-conditioned imagination.

The truth is, the deeper study of occultism is too rich, too vast; it demands so much from the individual, that only a hint, only a fragment is carefully given to the seeker, who often feels it is grudgingly given and not generously. This is not so. The bright unknowns who watch and compassionately guard the pilgrim, control the load and carry much of the burden till spiritual consciousness has matured; till sublimation and re-integration clarifies, and truths are comprehended in their undistorted importance; for would it be right for the child mind to be shown the purgatories and paradises of the cosmos?

Now before interest in occultism was reawakened, medievalism was in power; the books of light were sealed and in dust. Long winter froze the mind and Ignorance ruled the sad centuries, grew arrogant and the luminous hierarchies of Nature sank into memories of a peasants' folklore; and the great mysteries were riveted into the adamant of dogma.

Through the centuries freedom was a forbidden territory; only through secret devices could the mind attain spiritual wealth. Minds were homeless save in the narrow cell and enclosed cloisters where doctrines and rituals led one way only: to the narrow creeds of the Church.

Yet through the distance and the dust came the thrust and power of new deliverance, and through reason and the labour of Science dogmas were exploded. But the nobility of the new tyrannies began to reign; aristocrats of the practical: the bomb as an orb, the test-tube as the sceptre, and the chromium-plated wheel as the crown. All rituals of utility in the name of reason. "The old gods are dead; long live the new gods!"

Medievalism and its incense, its stained glass and vestments, its solemn intonings, is scattered! Now the light of reason reigns: a proud and powerful race of minds, but—barren because godless.

All life travails upon the rack of evolution, and only mechanical devices can give it comfort. As religion brought dusk to the mind of man, science would bring dawn. Science would disentangle and unravel, break open nature's box of tricks and make, for the first time, meaning from the discordant and uneconomic jumble of nature's blind gropings.

And the spirit of man? The fiery and imponderable spark that can neither be caught nor analysed? This was the unknowable, the non-existent, also the unnecessary;

the mythology of the primitive and the beliefs of the childhood of man. This was also the superficial interpretation given by muddled thinkers, who confused qualities with quantities. But this was in the adolescent age of science; that aggressive youthfulness when profound mysteries were solved by shallow certainties. Yet in the history of human progress, this dynamic dynasty was brief; for the impregnable fortress of reason had locked out intuition, that quality through which comes illumination.

Now the material sciences begin to grope beyond the blueprint. They have distilled and analysed and refined beyond all discoverable substances until they have reached—in a collective sense—the abyss about which the student of the mysteries has heard—that great darkness which is a leap to light. Newer schools of psychology have built a few ramshackle bridges; but the few discoveries have revealed greater complexities.

Yet though the physical sciences began with anthems of praise they are concluding with requiems of despair; for they had released the fiery furnaces of the atom and with it the menace of the irresponsible. To use the thunderbolts of nature man must be stronger than nature. Nature has her dignity and will protect herself behind her bright augoeides: for science has dissolved its foundations and now treads a firmament of fire.

The matrices of Nature are no longer accidental patterns but the vital alphabet of a cosmic tongue; difficult to decipher, yet becoming ever clearer as the intellectual method cooperates with the intuitive.

APHORISMS ON OBSERVATION

For he hath the blessings of Uriel and seeth high and low: the secret strength of adamant places and the source of the rafters of the rainbow. His sight is with the wing, the petal and the rock. His sight is in the heart of man and can weigh his sorrows; his sight can measure conceit and innocence. For he hath the blessings of Uriel the deep-sighted Angel.

The Universe is based on reason and mechanics. Its emptiness is only apparent; all is activity with meaning. And the spiritualised mind expects the unexpected. The commonplace scene may reveal a mystery; the air, a hidden pulsation; within stillness, great activities lapping the uppermost fringes of perception. The essences, stored in the vats of a profound consciousness, overflow, gush and cascade in rainbow richness till such a mind is enthroned in the blazonries and symbols of the cosmic archives.

To one with full awareness space is no longer empty; influences no longer invisible. The atmosphere pulsating and rhythmic and infinite in extension. The seed of an idea is seen almost simultaneously as a magnificent tree; ideas possess a royal richness.

There are no trivialities to the illuminated mind; all is significant. Size has no value; only quality and intensity. To observe with intensity is to dig deep; to observe shallowly is to be superficial however much information be obtained.

[*Occult Observer* (London), vol. 1, no. 2 (Summer 1949): pp. 104–06.]

To observe with the eye of the artist is to see pattern and colour, designs and harmonies; delicate nuances and all subtle shades in form. The untrained eye observes shapes and colours but cannot integrate and give them meaning. But the capacity to observe does not belong to the eyes alone; the ears observe, the touch, the taste: all these are doors to an expansion of consciousness. The difference between the artist and the intellectual is that the artist listens-in, the intellectual thinks it out.

The awareness of the animal brings appetites and desires. The awareness of the mind brings perspective and proportion. The awareness of the imagination brings a capacity for creation and patterns. All these harmonised through observation can lead to illumination.

When we attempt the final analysis of a term, we frequently admit defeat. If we bring to it a wide range of experience and thought, it changes like a chameleon; it has so many relationships, so many contradictions; yet upon such quicksands of thought we erect impressive structures of philosophy; chapels and cathedrals of theology, and the monotonous buildings of reason. Yet with all this activity we discover that we have but sharpened the instruments for analysis. Persistent probing, however, can lead to unanalysable certainties, those intuitions that are the observations of the soul.

As the capacity for observation becomes more highly trained, questions and replies, problems and solutions are almost simultaneously solved.

A fool can be intense, but the result can be only an emotional splash; yet the comprehensive intensity of a wise man can enrich permanently. Deep observation relates the apparently unrelatable. Herein lies the difference between the engineer and the inventor; they use similar material, but the inventor uses his head whilst the engineer uses his hands.

To observe demands flexibility of all perceptions. Habit and tradition show you what you expect to see; flexibility overflows such limitations and hence discoveries are made.

An idea is no use till it is like an illumination; till it grows in the consciousness as a force and an urge; as a necessity to be born; as a demonstrable fact.

To see without thinking is to have a starved mind; is to be a pauper amid riches; a beggar brain.

When observing always bear in mind the duality underlying all activity, and when disentangling these two states most problems may be solved.

Yet we are also observed. Few realise how we are watched and protected; otherwise the streets would be a shambles; our so-called lucky escapes, unlucky ones. Thus is the observer observed and—unless it is his destiny—protected.

QUAESTOR

THE MAN IN THE OCCULT STREET

Where is this street? And who is the man?

Every street and each individual man has a hidden counterpart. Hence the "man in the occult street" is one who attempts to find his way in the unfamiliar surroundings about which he has heard and read, but to which he has not found the entrance.

We all know the phrase: "What does the man in the street say?" We try to visualise an amorphous individual who has certain opinions; generally, to our way of thinking, utterly commonplace.

Now the man in the occult street has read many opinions about the mysteries, the path, initiation, masters, adepts, Mahatmas, Tibet, Egypt, and India . . . an immense flotsam and jetsam of traditional occult phraseology which lies stewing and fermenting in the great cauldron of the subconscious. To him, and for him, is a vast new literature and teaching for his spiritual digestion.

Where is this eager and hungry man going?

In the beginning he has an ingenuous and innocent attitude. He is so willing . . . so very eager . . . to travel this long pilgrimage, but he has no experience; his intuitions are clouded by the confused thinking of his teachers. He is willing to stand on his head; squat on his haunches; meditate in some vacuous manner upon impossible imagery; remain in a mental rain and in occasional emotional thunderbursts, bareheaded and bewildered, wondering where to run for refuge and guidance . . .

[*Occult Observer* (London), vol. 1, no. 3 (1949): pp. 129–30.]

only to meet equally dazed fellow-creatures who are seeking, as he is seeking, for refuge and understanding.

But here we come to the moment when he is the ordinary man in the street. He has found a few opinions, some vague hints about the Cosmos; he has picked some straws from the gutters of occult information, and with these little treasures he explains to others equally as ignorant the Sublime Meaning of Things. He becomes a trifle arrogant. He is the man in the street with definite opinions, with an impertinent air, and the strut of the egotistic nonentity. Now, however compassionate the gods, however willing to help, this attitude can finish, for that incarnation, his journey. One of the habits of the man in the street is to be attracted to crowds, and not to go his separate way. For the seeker can rarely find his true path or his true road unless he has the courage to travel fearlessly, examine the opinions of others honestly, and have a bigger comprehension than the average man in the street.

If he would tread the loftier altitudes that the true Teachers are only too anxious to reveal to the honest pilgrim, there is an occult road for each person. If he would travel fast, he must travel free. He must learn to discriminate the stupid from the wise; he must not accept the clamorous opinions of the mass; and he must be capable of disentangling his emotions from those about him. In that manner he will no longer be one of the grey nonentities of which the men of the street are composed.

WHAT IS A TRUTH?

"'What is truth?' asked jesting Pilate, but stayed not for an answer," says Bacon ("Of Truth"). It is also possible that he feared one.

The veils before a truth may be from one's own weaving: entangling strands of dishonesty, the glittering tinsels of egotism, sackcloths of stupidity; wrapping round wrapping, till one's world is a sluggish darkness. And for such there is neither enlightenment nor liberation; though the word *Truth* comes often to their lips.

If we creep round the mountains of our errors, we shall always remain on a low level. Heights are to be climbed, not avoided, if the search for a truth is honest.

A truth is a demonstrable imponderable.

What is a truth? What is my relationship to the universe? and to myself? the ethereal in me, the monster in me? For I am indefinite, confused, tangled in instincts and intuitions, a blur of localised sense-impressions submerged in the hot swamps of myself

Yet my intuition tells me there is a vague path leading out. But again, to discover a truth means release from one set of conditions to another set of unknown conditions. For truths do not free, they bring burdens; they give clear hearing, and a greater clamour is heard; they bring clear sight, and a greater confusion is seen. Truth does not set you free; it only makes you stand upright.

[*Occult Observer* (London), vol. 1, no. 3 (1949): pp. 183–85.]

To say "I seek truth" is to mean that I seek the roots of God. I seek beyond and beyond and beyond, an immortal mariner sailing infinity.

It seems that a truth has a shining surface and is buried behind a field of force; it is invisibly cushioned and repels enquiries and research, keeping the investigator at a distance. A truth avoids definition, yet teases the intuition and the intellect; for though it slips and eludes us it keeps us under control and forces its laws upon us. Our opinions and biases, our conceits and dishonesties make no impact upon a truth; it becomes more elusive—and when we lack intuitive understanding —which is a spiritual fact—we are further than ever from its power and light. Certain theologians when in darkness about the mechanics through which spiritual truths work use the word *Faith*.

The dishonest who would seek truth could more easily entice the reflection of sunlight on water; or winnow a shadow to find its virtue; refine the intangible, or pirouette in a vacuum.

What one wishes to know is not an explanation about our everyday practical activities but about our inner conditions, that are such profound mysteries.

The primitive is curious but dull; the scientist seeks practical solutions, but does not discover the origins hidden in the unknown. The intellectual seeks and gropes into philosophies, but the results are beggarly. Many use mysticism, some meditation; but few receive revelation, for the ultimate truths are forbidden.

QUAESTOR

MISLEADERS OF THE OCCULT

In ancient days in the Near East there were many priesthoods who taught in the Temples to selected students many of the Mysteries that today have apparently become common knowledge. Such would be the implications if many of the occult myths that are published had a basis in fact.

But with the disappearance of the Temples there has also come the disappearance of truth; and the urge and hunger of many interested, and of those who have some vague recollection of ancient Temple-teaching, are attracted to any kind of so-called occult literature as soon as published.

Now, in much of this occult literature there are contradictory systems, superficial interpretations, egotistic assumptions of individual revelations, impertinent claims and a muddy mass of twisted thought that can only lead to the position of the patient being much worse after the unskilled psychic doctor has administered ... often with the best of intentions ... his so-called cure.

Since the pagan priesthoods and their Temples were submerged by the rise of new religions, leaving behind the debris and job lots of gods and goddesses which later were incorporated in the new religions; centuries of persecution of those who strove to preserve the Old Knowledge has resulted in a vast ignorance concerning the true sources of spiritual activity and in almost utter obliviousness to man's relationship to the spiritual plan. This has opened the door to charlatans.

[*Occult Observer* (London), vol. 1, no. 4 (1950): pp. 193–94.]

This is a democratic age and Jack is as good as his master, and we speak of such things as the "classless society" and say that "all are equal." The result of such a creed is obvious. Anyone can rise and say that he has as much right to teach and to give forth whatever he imagines, whatever he wishes, whatever fantasy has entered his mind; and claim that such-and-such is the True Pattern of the Universe. They seek to confine the Cosmos in little chapels, strange churches and so-called Secret Schools wherein they claim for themselves the powers of the High Priest, and claim mysterious audiences with the Gods.

In olden days these so-called teachers would have been made to prove themselves before the Initiated High Priests who would know the claimants for what they were, and would place them in their degree accordingly, permitting them to teach only what was known to them according to the nature of their magical grade.

All this has been altered. First came religion, then came philosophy, then came science. Each veil removed the seeker a little further from the True Altar. Finally the seeker stood alone amid a turmoil and a darkness, wondering, in spite of his intuition, whether there ever was a Spiritual Pattern and a compassionate listener to the cries of his heart.

Why are so many so-called Occult Schools of such brief existence? They begin with remarkable systems. Books are published, headquarters established, enthusiasms roused, publicity is focussed upon them; many prophesies are made and unheard-of "Masters" appear in this Occult circus and orate. But alas ... not only is this "immortal" very mortal but also very ephemeral, and the thud of disappointed hopes can be heard by those who have gone through tests and endurances in other schools. It is strange. Surely a true prophet and illuminated mind will only build upon the permanent rock of established truth?

DIOGENES AND THE OCCULTIST

We all know Diogenes was a Greek Philosopher who lived in a tub and walked about with a lamp looking for an honest man. To the anchorite this is an original and admirable condition of life; for here was one who had developed the capacity to do without to such a degree that, with only a slight difference, one could live almost as comfortably in a coffin: the spiritual idea being to dispense with the riches of this world until only rags and a few planks were sufficient. There is little difference between the tramp who has nothing and the psychological tramp who wants nothing. The important question is whether wanting nothing is a virtue and suggests progress of a spiritual kind, or whether it signifies complete lack of interest in worldly things?

To make a virtue of a lack is not truly honest, though it may he accepted patiently; but one should ask oneself why does the cultured person wish—whenever possible—to surround himself with lovely things? Does this prove he is lower than he who is satisfied with bare walls, water and a crust of bread?

The highly sensitive, mature person feels hunger for lovely things and whenever possible attempts to purchase pictures or books. All those forms of art he considers to be doors leading to other realms of beauty; this hunger would not be there if a recollection of these things had not been in his memory either through past lives or through recollections of higher realms to which he travels in sleep.

[*Occult Observer* (London), vol. 1, no. 6 (1950): pp. 337–38.]

Hence one can see that a Diogenes or the unkempt hermit, the fervent anchorite or the ascetic, expresses an arid and unimaginative outlook; for if the saying "as above so below" is true, a material pauperism can be but an expression of spiritual pauperism.

Reviews and Other Writings

BOOK REVIEWS

M. *THE DAYSPRING OF YOUTH*. LONDON AND
NEW YORK: PUTNAM, 1933.

["A New Yoga System," *Occult Review* (London), vol. 58, no. 2
(August 1933): pp. 114–17.]

In an age of economic earthquakes, when the security
of individuals and institutions is everywhere threatened,
it is obvious that civilisation is entering a new phase.
Many views as to the directing forces at work have
been put forward, such as the scientific and the social-
istic, but the spiritual aspect of the underlying causes
has been presented only by the occultist and mystic.

Humanity is entering a new age, a Springtide of
mental vitality, when youth will take precedence. In
this new age youth will be intolerant of old traditions
and beliefs; for it will be impatient for the spiritual
harmony that is to come to a planet now shaken by
chaos and hate.

In a work entitled *The Dayspring of Youth*, by M., a
new viewpoint is offered for the student of the West
who feels that Eastern occult doctrines are unsuited
to his modern outlook. The author gives a series of
yogi exercises and explains how the student can har-
monise himself with the new vibrations now entering
the world's atmosphere.

As in science time brings progress, so it is in the
world of occultism; and I feel that an important addi-
tion to occult literature has been made in the publica-
tion of this book.

Many occult works mention the mental body; but
few, if any, have given a detailed description of its anat-
omy and of its relationship to the physical body; and

rarely have we been told what actually occurs on the mental levels when the student meditates. Here the author describes the slow building up, by yoga, of a mental screen, called "the Silver Shield." This Shield protects the student from foreign mental impacts, thus giving him the power to enter his own true world of being—that inner universe he has built up through the experiences of countless elemental and physical incarnations.

"The macrocosm in the microcosm" is a phrase frequently used in occultism, though little has been said as to the method whereby one may discover one's own vast potentialities. The higher consciousness in man is rarely manifested: only the illusory self is known. In this work one is shown how to realise these great potentialities and gain that emancipation for which one hungers, but which is scarcely ever attained.

The student has probably heard much about Nature's consciousness; but how to enter her dynamic realms and become initiated into her mysteries has rarely been revealed. Much in this book will seem fantastic to those who study this subject for the first time; but it should be remembered that the fantasies of today are the facts of tomorrow.

Primarily the work deals with the collective consciousness within man, the method whereby these can be tapped, and how the power to respond to their sovereign intelligence—called "the Innermost"—may be developed.

Many students know that the physical body is composed of atomic intelligences, but few are aware of a method whereby they can contact these minute entities and learn of their wisdom. Here the author shows, clearly and logically, how the student can tap his inner sources of information not only of the past, but also entities belonging to those higher phases of his being that have evolved beyond his present realm.

Owing to the different psychologies, climatic conditions and changes in earth-currents, the Western body is unfitted for Eastern yoga practices. Yet few Western students know that the Occident possesses its own secret doctrine and methods of spiritual unfoldment. Much in this work should be of vital importance to the enquirer. Intellectually he may believe that he lives in a world of illusion; but to realise this is another matter. To enter his own world of being and discover his true place and part in the great work of man and nature is an experience given to few. Yet this book endeavours to show how, if a man will but work hard and be persistent enough, he can unlock his divine inheritance and help to bring peace and wisdom to a troubled and despairing world.

In the following extracts the nature of some of the practical methods advocated may be seen.

A torn mental screen brings disease and often insanity; for in this wound hordes of atoms and entities find a place to build their structures, and in some desperate cases we have found several colonies adhering to the envelope. In this manner they can speak into the mind of the subject and the normal personality is often replaced by others. These severe cases can be healed by proper care and judgment by the doctor; but he must be able to locate the cause and not judge it objectively. The coming century will produce a new school that will deal with such cases successfully, and a mind harassed by such conditions will greatly benefit if the patient can live in a very high altitude; for such atoms and entities cannot rise owing to their density and weight. . . .

The mental screen is often bent from its normal shape if the tissues of the body are destroyed and will appear like an elongated balloon, and when the body is unable to radiate into the mental screen a hollow depression is seen. This tells the developed student what organ is diseased. A sudden fall or shock can sometimes injure a membrane of this screen, and some period will elapse ere it will return to its normal shape. . . .

From year to year the thought-waves about us are increasing, and this pressure upon humanity brings an ever-increasing agitation to sensitive minds. It is by aspiration that we protect ourselves from this thought-bombardment. Hence it is imperative to erect a protective shield about these node points. This bombardment is caused by man's uncontrolled thought-agitation that will later return and inflict him with certain forms of mental disorders. The rapid voltage of the Dayspring of Youth will add to this state of mind. War has also loosened conditions that seek to destroy the healthy mind. (pp. 162–64)

The long chapter on the elemental world is illuminating, inasmuch as a description of each kingdom is given, embodying information never before recorded. The West knows little about the play of elemental forces through its civilisations and their part in human evolution

In occult and theosophical works much has been written about the "Brothers" or "Masters." In the present work the American student will learn something that should interest him profoundly; for mention is made of "the Great Atlantean," the "Brother" or "Master" who presides over the American commonwealth. At present the student's country is in travail. Mighty forces are guiding the destiny of that land towards and era of mental and spiritual expansion that will eventually make it a pioneer in the expression of the Dayspring of Youth.

The scope of the volume unfortunately makes it necessary that the treatment of a number of subjects, such as Atlantis, the Sphinx, and Lemuria should be fragmentary.

The chapter concerning the submerged worlds should give those interested in Spiritualism much to think over.

Many occult works speak of the Higher Self; but man's *elemental* Higher Self has either been ignored or not known. An analysis is given of both, and the nature of their work in man's development is described. Also, what actually occurs when the student awakens the Kundalini, or Solar Force, is dealt with in detail.

This book demands concentration and study; but the results should give the reader a clearer vision of the hidden framework of the universe and clear up many misconceptions. The glossary of new terms and definitions should also help greatly.

For a new age, a new method. Only by adapting and harmonising ourselves to the new forces now entering the world and man's atmosphere can students become the pioneers for the Dayspring of Youth.

MICHAUD, J. *OCCULT ENIGMAS: A SERIES OF METAPHYSICAL INVESTIGATIONS.* LONDON: UMA PRESS, 1939.

[*Occult Review* (London), vol. 66, no. 4 (October 1939): p. 255]

Here is an important contribution to occult literature, vividly and vitally written. This is no two-dimensional work of what the author has heard and has thought, but of what he has experienced, producing a depth of understanding rarely found in works of this nature.

Many passages are floridly written; but as this furbelowed style is the result of a high-spirited mind teeming with ideas and profound scholarship it is a fault one would wish to see in many of today's occult publications.

Occult Enigmas has been planned as a series of twelve talks wherein each subject is given a chapter. These include "The Work of the Masters"; "Karma"; "The Astral World"; "Magic"; "Alchemy"; etc., etc. But the author has threaded each subject with so many quotations that the result is a sparkling, fascinating pattern.

The reader should obtain many fresh, startling angles upon Occultism form this work, though, as truth is too variable a state, many of Dr. Michaud's solutions may not satisfy the ever-probing mind of the serious student, for ultimately an understanding of the Great Mysteries does depend upon the degree of development of the seeker.

Nevertheless to read this book is an experience, and the student will undoubtedly obtain some solutions to some of his "Occult Enigmas."

STEWART, C. R. *THE DIVINE VISION: A KEY TO THE GREATER MYSTERIES.* LONDON: M. HOUGHTON, 1939
["Introduction," pp. 5–8]

What are the essential qualities necessary for a work upon Occultism? The message should be important; the style clear and simple; and the subject should illuminate the mind of the reader. Unfortunately, such qualities are rarely found among the numerous books upon Occultism published today. We believe that C.R. Stewart, who died some years ago, and who is the author of this work, has woven such qualities within *The Divine Vision*. One feels he had experienced much about which he wrote, and therein lies the importance of this work. He describes the various phases of consciousness through which he passed, and the knowledge gained from them, in such a manner that the reader feels that here is one who as attained a clear conception of the universe and the forces flowing through it.

His suggestions upon meditation are excellent: they are direct and should produce results. There is no suggestion that the student should contort his limbs into impossible postures in order to unveil the secret teachings and solve the Divine Mysteries. Truth is not hidden from man if he fails to meditate upon his navel, or place the sole of his foot beneath his rectum. If the student wishes to awaken such psychic forces—which he will finally have to discard if he studies Occultism seriously —he will not find this book useful. But if the student has serious aspirations and desires to serve humanity, these teachings will be invaluable.

Today there are so many systems of training; so many schools; so many teachers who claim infallibility, that only by the development of the intuitive faculty can the seeker hope to contact his own reality and become aware of his place in the divine patter. It is this development of the intuition that C.R. Stewart emphasises.

The section dealing with the Christ-myth may not appeal to those to whom the Christ was a historical figure; for this human touch brings comfort to many, yet the author believes his contention to be of primary importance. As he says, his findings are not original, but they confirm—through his intuitional development— much that harmonises with his discoveries concerning the true significance of the Mysteries. The following paragraph may show why the author has given this matter so much attention:

> But this does not in the least detract from the value of the gospel teachings, for all truths are inspired by the Spirit of Divine Wisdom, and the human channel through which they come is immaterial. The modern tendency is too often to magnify the person of the supposed teacher while ignoring the message. (pp. 46–47.)

The author's attack upon the pseudo-occult schools should be welcomed by those students to whom the ideal is of greater value than the individual. That many schools are doing important work is agreed, but, unfortunately, certain schools use systems that are deadly in their results. Much is unintentional on the part of the teachers; but few of them work consciously from the highest states of human development, and their limitations react upon their disciples.

A great truth, simply expressed, may seem bleak to the reader seeking a florid and complicated description; yet such a quality of directness possesses the force of an arrow. Unhappily, much occult literature is the expansion of a simple problem wherein the student's mind is sent drifting diffusedly over numerous unrelated subjects. Yet in this short work there are a series of simple statements out of which a new school of occult thought could be founded.

The student will probably, and rightly, ask where did the author obtain his material? One can only suggest that if the student will follow certain practices laid down in this book, he may also discover the source;

for it is in the development of the intuition that realisation comes, and, although I do not claim to have followed out the system C.R. Stewart describes, yet similar methods were taught me wherein aspiration was the keynote.

In but a few paragraphs he clarifies the somewhat muddled ideas many have about the differences between Occultism and Mysticism. His explanation on the awakening of the Kundalini is also most important, as so many teachings which concentrate upon the development of this centre frequently result in nervous disorders in the pupil.

This work should help the student to discover that there are no short-cuts in Occultism, and that the most complicated ritualisms and formulas may have to be discarded, and with them many theories. Illumination —the opening of a door in the consciousness—cannot be forced as a burglar forces the door of a safe. Though he may have awakened some psychic centres through certain practices, we feel that this work will show him a loftier purpose, and because of this *The Divine Vision* should be considered an important contribution to occult literature.

It is true that C.R. Stewart makes a number of statements concerning the interior planes readers can neither prove nor disprove; yet, in spite of this, the practical suggestions regarding meditations, intuition, and the common-sense definitions of occult terms can become demonstrable if the student will follow the methods laid down in this book.

In conclusion, here is a simple system, a warning what to avoid and a hope that by following the author's suggestions the student may attain an ever-increasing illumination into the Great Mysteries.

GEDGE, GILBERT HENRY. *LETTERS TO A YOUNG BUSINESS MAN.* FOREWORD BY HENRY THOMAS HAMBLIN. LONDON: C. W. DANIEL, [1939]

[*Occult Review* (London), vol. 67, no. 1 (January 1940): p. 22]

Here are a series of sincere letters wherein the author suggests that genuine Christian principles can be made to harmonise with one's business practice. A book that should help the religious-minded youth with a business career before him.

COLE, MAWBY T. AND VERA CARSON REID. *GODS IN THE MAKING: MAN AND THE LAW OF CONTINUITY.* LONDON: A. DAKERS, 1936.

[*Occult Review* (London), vol. 67, no. 1 (January 1940): p. 30]

This is a profound philosophic work without the tormented philosophic jargon so frequently used in such literature. The authors have expressed some of the fundamental principles of divine evolution in a simple and easy manner. It is ambitious; for the authors discuss man's relationship to the world, to all phases of consciousness, and to the universe in its deepest manifestation. And they do this well. It is clear and concise, and, though a small book, should satisfy the most scientific mind in its methods of tracing the life-force through the mineral, vegetable, animal and human kingdoms; then into the slow unfoldment of cosmic consciousness. The occult student will intuitively recognise the truths written here; for this is not alone an intellectual work: spiritual experiences have been woven through it.

Any group studying occultism will find this useful as a textbook. The authors have a most comprehensive grasp of occult doctrine, particularly the section entitled "Man to Gods." The chapters devoted to the astrological significance of the Aquarian Age into which humanity is now entering should greatly interest the astrologer. This book is a definite contribution to modern occultism.

O'DONNELL, ELLIOTT. *HAUNTED CHURCHES*.
LONDON: QUALITY PRESS, [1939].

[*Occult Review* (London), vol. 67, no. 1 (January 1940): p. 59]

Here are more than just vague descriptions of hauntings from the literature of ghostland; quite a few are first-hand; for besides being a specialist in this subject the author has also been a ghost-hunter for many years, and he has carefully collected the most unusual happenings. Some tales have an Oriental flavour; attempting to seal a ghost in a bottle and casting it into a pond is one. Another tale is similar except that a phantom bull is compressed into a bottle and likewise sunk. Perhaps this is the origin of Oxo. But not all the ghosts are terrifying or fantastic: some are pitiful, and ghosts that are homeless on both sides of the veil are pitiful indeed. The Halloween incidents wherein a modern witch clad in a gown covered with demons and black cats, and carrying a broomstick whilst she waited for the author and some friends at King's Cross station, is very entertaining. The sequels were plentiful, but none were supernatural. Elliot O'Donnell has provided another most readable work for the seeker after ghostly happenings.

THOMAS, REV. C. DRAYTON. *AN AMAZING EXPERIMENT*. LONDON: LECTURES UNIVERSAL, [1936]

[*Occult Review* (London), vol. 68, no. 2 (April 1940): p. 127]

This is a thorough piece of psychical investigation

concerning messages from the spirit of a child transmitted to distant strangers. This account includes some very interesting photographs and is a painstaking record in proof of survival. Should interest the student of psychical phenomena.

THOMAS, REV. C. DRAYTON. *IN THE DAWN BEYOND DEATH*. LONDON: LECTURES UNIVERSAL, [1936]

[*Occult Review* (London), vol. 67, no. 4 (October 1940): p. 184]

The Spiritualist will find this modest book exceedingly encouraging, as the messages from those who have passed over are vivid and convincing. Some are most thought-provoking, and nearly each conversation conveys some interesting aspect of these psychic worlds. Mrs. Osborne Leonard is the medium.

THREE FAMOUS MYSTICS: ST. MARTIN BY A. E. WAITE; JACOB BOEHME BY W. P. SWAINSON; SWEDENBORG BY W. P. SWAINSON. LONDON: RIDER, [1939]. *THREE FAMOUS ALCHEMISTS: RAYMOND LULLY BY A. E. WAITE; CORNELIUS AGRIPPA BY LEWIS SPENCE; PARACELSUS BY W. P. SWAINSON*. LONDON: RIDER, [1939]. *THREE FAMOUS OCCULTISTS: DR. JOHN DEE BY G. M. HORT; FRANZ ANTON MESMER BY R. B. INCE; THOMAS LAKE HARRIS BY W. P. SWAINSON*. LONDON: RIDER, [1939]

[*Occult Review* (London), vol. 68, no. 2 (April 1940): p. 86]

Many students have heard, at some time or another, about the above-mentioned great names in occultism and mysticism, yet few short biographies have been written giving a satisfactory and sympathetic study of these men. It is here that the publishers have performed a useful service; for the writers chosen have done their work well: clarifying the teachings in such a manner that the reader will obtain a comprehensive understanding of their philosophies without having to struggle through numerous and heavy volumes. One feels that the authors have researched so thoroughly into these doctrines that they are fully competent to write about them. It will be noticed that the studies are well chosen, as each teacher has contributed some important aspect to these divine sciences.

One hopes that the publishers will continue these series in the future; for many more great names come to mind worthy of being recorded in these very useful and important biographies and teachings.

ORWELL, GEORGE. *NINETEEN EIGHTY-FOUR.*
LONDON: SECKER AND WARBURG, [1949]

[*Occult Observer* (London), vol. 1, no. 2 (Summer 1949): pp. 124–25]

The above is the logical work arising from a defeated economic idealism. In George Orwell's book the principle of Evil reaches its climax: a terrible indictment of a despiritualised and Godless state of society: one of many books now published revealing a dawning revulsion against a growing bureaucracy. Though a monstrous fantasy, it possesses a subconscious relationship to the lower astral hells.

George Orwell has discovered certain truths, but only the dark half of them, the paradoxical teachings of the Tao.

This is an important book; a prophecy and a warning that a materialistic Utopia can lead to the greatest tyranny of all: a lust for power to dominate every form of nobility without fear of any ultimate punishment.

The brutalising crescendo and cynical conclusion

will leave the reader with a sense of alarm and futility: here is no light, no hope, no bearable future; a sense of eternal psychological darkness where Evil dominates all, where progress is paralysed. It seems that after the glow of the red light our intellectual begins to perceive the black light: an abyss into which science is leading society. Man cannot stand still, and economic ease leads to greater confusions and greeds: inflating the stomach and diffusing man's leisure into childish pastimes add nothing to culture, but make man an easy victim to growing psychological diseases till, as George Orwell sees, all mankind is gripped by a planetary insanity where lies and truths and good and bad mean the same; where two and two make five, and where there is no history, facts being deliberately entangled and distorted into the texture of man's consciousness.

This is a bitter book, emerging from a frustrated heart and mind that does not acknowledge nor believe in the personal immortality of man, whose idealism has gone sour; and who is not intuitively aware that beyond the intellectual boundaries many have received nobler intimations of consciousness, and that beyond our small individual experiences are greater beings above as well as below who watch and comprehend our struggles, and who may—using natural laws—play their subtle parts in our everyday activities.

The dogmas of materialism are as bad as the dogmas of any Church. It is possible that the blueprints of a bureaucracy might lead to George Orwell's monstrous conclusions, or, before that, to suicide of society through the atom bomb. Yet there is the third way: the middle way, the way of the Tao, the way of balance, wherein one can see the eternal paradoxes but with an illuminated understanding.

HESSE, HERMAN. *MAGISTER LUDI.*
TRANSLATED FROM THE GERMAN BY MERVYN
SAVILL. LONDON: ALDUS; NEW YORK:
FREDERICK UNGAR, 1949

[*Occult Observer* (London), vol. 1, no. 2 (Summer 1949): pp. 125–26]

(A lengthy work, and therefore impossible to give it a comprehensible review in our limited space.)

Scene, A.D. 2000. Again the dark ages after a terrifying war and a great medieval darkness; but here is a nobler understanding of man's relationships: man a spiritual being.

Magister Ludi or the Bead Game is apparently the cultured synthesis of all the arts. One might translate this as the awareness of all the microcosmic activities and the dynamic details of an inner cosmic consciousness.

Again we come to the eternal dualism; but here it is mature, and spiritualised.

Joseph Knecht is one who obviously reaches mastership—one who has attained a cosmic consciousness; who has the permanent spiritual vision and full control. This work's symbolic patterns and poetic sensitivity is highly original; the magical quality of music; the powers o f association and harmonious blendings of all elements and matters.

Of great interest to the student in Occultism are the posthumous writings of a Master, wherein are related the stories of three incarnations: the Rainmakers, the Father Confessor and the Indian Life.

Music seems to be the integrating influence, but one might symbolise all the philosophic descriptions as the spiritual game of life; but not in the shallow emotionalism of most, but in the deeper sense of the divine pilgrimist and the attainment of super-control.

The author reveals very considerable scholarship

and reading in numerous facets of occult doctrine and the arts.

Here the nature of man's possibilities is pitched very high, and through a leisurely and dignified pilgrimage Joseph Knecht reaches a spiritual maturity and then realises still greater ascents before him.

Hermann Hesse's world of the future shows nobility and the justification of man's existence on this planet.

MICHAUD, J. *SYMPHONIE FANTASTIQUE: DIABLERIE IN FOUR MOVEMENTS; A SYMPHONY IN WORDS*. LONDON: UMA PRESS, 1949

[*Occult Observer* (London), vol. i, no. 3 (1949): pp. 189–90]

Here is a new and important work upon vital occult teachings.

Beginning with an astonishingly detailed description of the inner spiritual or higher astral appearances of trees and their magical healing qualities, and revealing methods of curing some of man's deadliest diseases, this book should be read by every genuine student for whom so much mystical literature is written but who receives little which deals with Nature's great laws and her techniques.

The setting is most original. Two children, Dolci and Farni, escaping a storm, seek shelter and fall asleep in a ruined castle; but, on awaking to their Higher Selves in full consciousness, find they are in hell amid grotesque imps and monsters who make them captive by the command of Lucifer who rules this realm.

Throughout the colourful dialogue that follows between Lucifer, his foul imps and the divine children are interspersed important teachings from which the intuitive and the initiated will learn much.

The language is as fantastic as the subject, and, though not a lengthy work, it reveals to the reader so many facets of the mysteries that the student will re-read this work many times, always discovering something new. Works of spiritual power are like bridges between the spiritual kingdoms and the earthly ones: the reader can cross again and again, receiving a renewal of spiritual strength.

One might describe this work as a mystical romp where the eternal battle between light and dark is fought in musical terms; many of Lucifer's friends and servants are given such names as Rotondo, Phonascus, Zoppo, Staccato, Gachuco and Quint.

The solemn-minded reader who is out-of-tune within himself will not enjoy this work; though if he will per-severe he may discover highly-charged voltages of great occult truths. The lugubrious-faced puritan of occult-ism, to whom laughter seems blasphemous, will wince many times at the author's occasional slanginess, but this really only reveals a mind at home and at ease in matters of a spiritual nature.

This is undoubtedly a great book.

It is divided into four movements, and is in the form of a play. Almost every musical term is used, including description of numerous historical and modern instru-ments, in an amazing dance and bacchanal as it races to a climax in a mad medley before Lucifer. The fourth and final movement rises to an inspired climax: a de-scription of the warriors from the cosmos, again in the great battle; the planetary gods and their soldiers at-tacking the castle of hell and their weird and distorted inhabitants under their fallen god Lucifer.

Symphonie Fantastique will puzzle many readers of

the occult who will probably ask why the author has used musical terminology; but when we fully realise that all forms of matter are but vibrations and that all forms are part of a universal orchestration, the reader will appreciate the significance of this original work.

Certain great mysteries have been explained that should clear many confusions in occult belief, and the beautiful revelation about affinities should illuminate the minds of the honest seekers.

In addition, this work is a significant and noble addition to literature; it will be read when the muddled and dull stuff of occult theory is forgotten. For though entitled *Symphonie Fantastique* there are in it more correct descriptions of spiritual appearances than in many detailed works of non-existent states written by the scissor-and-paste occultist.

Yes, this is a great work. Beyond its fantasy gleams a very great light.

MICHAUD, J. *THE BOOK OF SA-HETI*. LONDON: UMA PRESS, 1950

[*Occult Observer* (London), vol. 1, no. 5 (1950): pp. 331–32]

A Holy Book has been written. The reviewer of the above work can find no simpler and clearer description than this and is fully aware of the significance of such a term, yet feels justified in considering that this work possesses such qualities.

The author has taken from the Vishnu Puranas the tale of Chrishna-Jeseus, Arjuna and Maia, actual names in these ancient scriptures, which became John and Mary, also the various episodes incorporated in the New Testament 3,000 years later, and developed these incidents in so sublime a language that the reviewer could not lay this work down until finished. The author brings such fire and power, such a blaze of beauty from a remote past that the reader will again relive this enchantment and feel he has been blessed with a spiritual exaltation.

This is a work; of great illumination ; consistently inspired from first to final page. In wisdom and in vision, power flows from the mind as though it had been lifted up and the true mystical teachings revealed as when first given forth 5,000 years ago. All is living : the warm rainbow hues of ancient India, its birds and beasts and flowers: the evil and the good people; the astonishing magical battles; the holy and benign beings who teach the true wisdom and prophecy; the panoramas of the higher and lower realms ; the various gates of the Paradises and the Hells. Again the great mystical teachings; unperverted, radiant with the truths like flaming jewels set in enamels and arabesques of words, to shine within the higher mind and set it alight. Here is an intense spiritual adventure for the sensitive and a living loveliness for every kind of reader.

This is a royal book : as though the Lord of the high-realm had inspired the writer to renew again the forsaken wisdom ; the kingly teachings that are true teachings in these days of a planetary Gethsemane when the great truths are crucified, and the illuminated minds dwell within a long Calvary.

This book will raise the hiss of the malicious and the snarling of those who have perverted the great issues of man's pilgrimage.

EDITORIAL

In the belief that a Catalogue should be more than columns of titles and descriptions we have added various essays and verse to make—we hope—the mental journey somewhat more interesting; though we feel that Occultism and its allied subjects are in themselves sufficiently important.

For those who have had occult experiences in a lesser or greater degree many of the works herein printed should evoke memories of those unknown and invisible places of activity that are the source of all objective phenomena.

To the beginner in matters Psychical and Occult, here is a varied and wide selection of works dealing with systems and philosophies, rituals and techniques that should contribute a widening of knowledge and ultimate expansion of consciousness that is the potential and dynamic inheritance of mankind.

p.s.—As we contemplate publishing an occult quarterly at some future date, we would appreciate comments from you.

[*Catalogue and Review* (London: Atlantis Bookshop, 1947), p. 2.]

TO OUR READERS

We are all units in an eternal pilgrimage, though few are aware of a plan or purpose or of the existence of the arcane sciences behind this phenomenal world; but to those who do believe they are brethren of spiritual dynasties the study of Occultism is of primary importance.

The *Occult Observer* will endeavour to maintain a high standard in its literature, in its thought and in its vision.

For many years occultism has been the hunting ground for confusing systems, unworkable techniques and grotesque interpretations of those levels beyond man's normal and limited vision. Therefore we hope whenever possible to publish and review such subjects as may disentangle the vast phantasmagoria misnamed occultism and bring a sense of proportion to these secret sciences of the illuminated.

Many articles in this first number concern psychological and artistic matters; for one of the noblest approaches to the study of man's fuller consciousness lies through the arts; avenues of awareness leading to great moments of revelation.

There is much controversial literature in occultism, and also much shallow and shoddy thought; because of this we shall endeavour to publish in future numbers only material either relating to the purely demonstrable technique in occult study or those visions revealing clearer understanding of the deeper purposes of man and the cosmos.

[*Occult Observer* (London), vol. 1, no. 1 (May 1949): p. 1.]

BIBLIOGRAPHY

The following list of works is intended to help the reader interested in following up on a particular passage or exploring more thoroughly the works of those authors cited in the main text. It is not suggested that these are the exact editions used by Juste.

Bacon, Francis. "Of Truth." In *Of the Literary and Professional Works*, pp. 81–84. Vol. 12, pt. 2 of The Works of Francis Bacon, collected and edited by James Spedding, Robert Leslie Ellis, and Douglas Denon Heath. Boston: Brown and Taggard, 1860.

Carroll, Lewis. *Alice's Adventures in Wonderland.* London: Macmillan, 1865. [Reprinted countless times by numerous publishers.]

Henley, William Ernest. "Invictus." In *Poems*, pp. 83–84. London: Macmillan, 1926. [The poem appears herein untitled.]

Kipling, Rudyard. "Recessional." In *The Five Nations, The Years Between, and Poems from History*, pp. 201–02. Vol. 23 of The Writings in Prose and Verse of Rudyard Kipling. New York: Charles Scribner's Sons, 1920.

Tennyson, Alfred Lord. "Crossing the Bar." In *The Works of Alfred Lord Tennyson*, annotated by Alfred Lord Tennyson, edited by Hallam Lord Tennyson, vol. 5, p. 102. Eversley Edition. New York: Macmillan, 1908

————. "Locksley Hall." In *The Works of Alfred Lord Tennyson*, annotated by Alfred Lord Tennyson, edited by Hallam Lord Tennyson, vol. 1, pp. 347–63. Eversley Edition. New York: Macmillan, 1908.